CHINA FROM EMPIRE TO NATION-STATE

China from Empire to Nation-State

WANG HUI

Translated by
MICHAEL GIBBS HILL

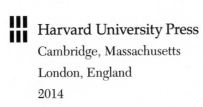
Harvard University Press
Cambridge, Massachusetts
London, England
2014

First printing

Originally published as the Introduction to *Zhongguo xiandai siziangde xingqi*, 2004, 2008
by SDX Joint Publishing Company, Beijing.

Library of Congress Cataloging-in-Publication Data

Wang, Hui, 1959–
   [Di guo yu guo jia. English]
   China from empire to nation-state / Wang Hui ; translated by Michael Gibbs Hill.
      pages cm
   Includes bibliographical references and index.
   ISBN 978-0-674-04695-5 (alk. paper)
  1. China—Civilization—Philosophy.   I. Title.
   DS721.W337 13513 2014
   951—dc23

                                       2014002578

Contents

TRANSLATOR'S INTRODUCTION   vii

China from Empire to Nation-State   1

1   Two Narratives of China and Their Derivative Forms   3

2   The Empire/Nation-State Binary and European
    "World History"   30

3   Heavenly Principle/Universal Principle and History   61

4   China's Modern Identity and the Transformation
    of Empire   101

    NOTES   147

    INDEX   171

Translator's Introduction

Wang Hui's writings on the history of modern China and life in the contemporary People's Republic have already gained a substantial audience in the English-speaking world.[1] His four-volume *Rise of Modern Chinese Thought* (*Xiandai Zhongguo sixiangde xingqi*, 2004), however, has gone untranslated in English for nearly a decade, despite extensive discussion of its contents.[2]

This book offers a modest, though not complete, remedy to that problem. The text translated in this volume, which is the introduction, or overview *(daolun)*, to *The Rise of Modern Chinese Thought*, explores many of the main questions covered in the full text. At some 90,000 characters in Chinese, it stands on its own as an important contribution to debates about the historiography of the past thousand years of Chinese history. Wang Hui begins with two simple, giant questions: How do we understand "China," and how do we understand "modernity" and the "modern"? Whereas many parts of the full four-volume work delve far into sources from Chinese intellectual and social history, the present text spends more time engaging with Japanese- and English-language scholarship on China and with the major theories of the historical development of capitalism found in the works of thinkers such as Adam Smith, G. W. F. Hegel, Karl Marx, Vladimir Lenin, and others. The breadth of Wang's discussion ensures that *China from Empire to Nation-State* will appeal to students and readers well outside of the academic specializations of Chinese history or Asian studies.

Section 1, "Two Narratives of China and Their Derivative Forms," shows how major strands of North American, Chinese, and Japanese scholarship all frame the Qing dynasty and the states that followed it under the rubric of "empire" or "nation-state"; implicit in all of these accounts is the notion that China cannot have a fully modern culture, society, or politics until the so-called transition from empire to nation-state is complete. Wang extends this discussion of the empire/nation-state binary to recent scholarly debates about Chinese (or Qing-dynasty) imperialism and colonialism, arguing that in many cases these studies overlook the tangled historical relations between capitalism, imperialism, and colonialism, and therefore fail to account fully for the diversity of historical experience in the polity we call "China," whether during the Qing or in the contemporary period. (A provocative extension of this argument, written after the publication of *The Rise of Modern Chinese Thought,* can be found in Wang's discussion of the status of Tibet as part of the People's Republic of China.)[3]

In the second section, "The Empire/Nation-State Binary and European 'World History,'" Wang Hui examines the emergence of images of China (and particularly the Qing dynasty) as a static empire congenitally unsuited both to the political form of the modern nation-state and to modern capitalism. This section highlights a particular problem of translation that can be traced to the establishment in the nineteenth century of (to use Lydia Liu's phrasing) "tropes of equivalence"[4] between the Chinese term *diguo,* the English term "empire," and the Japanese term *teikoku* ("empire"). Wang suggests that the image of non-European empires inherited from nineteenth-century Western European "world history" suppresses a long history of political and policy debate in China, especially discussions that surrounded systems of decentralized enfeoffment (*feng jian*) and centralized administration (*junxian*) as well as the flexible means by which the imperial court dealt with territories outside of China proper. Only when narratives of Chinese dynasties are removed from the "empire/nation-state binary," Wang argues, will it be possible to gain a new understanding of the richness of these historical dynamics and their relevance for the People's Republic.

Section 3, "Heavenly Principle/Universal Principle and History," outlines the transformation of *li* ("principle"), a central concept in Chinese thought, from the "Heavenly Principle" *(tianli)* of Song-dynasty neo-Confucianism to the axiomatic "Universal Principle" *(gongli)* that gained dominance at the turn of the twentieth century. Whereas the previous section emphasizes the importance of debates about political organization—such as enfeoffment versus centralized administration—as a resource for understanding modern China's predicament, Wang's history of Heavenly Principle focuses on an important "premodern" complex of concepts that is ignored in histories of modern China or, at best, valued only for its ability or inability to contribute to development toward modernity. Wang Hui refutes two common accounts of Heavenly Principle: on the one hand, early twentieth-century Chinese scholars (especially those associated with the May Fourth Movement) dismissed Heavenly Principle as just another part of what they saw as premodern China's irredeemably backward culture; on the other hand, the Kyoto School tended to see the establishment of the worldview of Heavenly Principle as a turn toward secularism, treating it as another sign of the development of a protomodern nationalism during the Song dynasty. Wang argues, however, that Heavenly Principle served as a site of debate and contestation between many different parties, as an idea to which both rulers and the ruled could appeal in support of a range of political and cultural positions.

The collapse of the worldview of Heavenly Principle did not, however, result in its disappearance. Wang suggests that the obsession with *discontinuity* in discussions of Heavenly Principle continued to structure the worldview of Universal Principle in important ways: whereas the discontinuity emphasized by Heavenly Principle also pointed to possibilities for aspects of ancient ideas and practices, the discontinuity emphasized by Universal Principle put forward a teleological view of development that depended on an irrevocable break from the past. This emphasis on the way consciousness of discontinuity links Heavenly Principle and Universal Principle to each other allows us to reconsider the significance of many aspects of neo-Confucian thought without simply reifying them as "sprouts of capitalism" or roadblocks to modernity. Of this attempt to avoid these pitfalls of historical analysis, Wang writes:

> [My purpose] was not to write a book clarifying the origins of modern Chinese intellectual history. What is a "rise"? Aside from the implication of "origin" embedded in this term, it can also be understood as "production and reproduction" (*shengsheng*), of "production and reproduction mean change" (*shengsheng zhi wei yi*), which, according to the *Book of Changes,* is a process full of change and development. . . . What I try to develop through my interpretation . . . may be called a perception framework of history, which is different from temporal teleology and is embedded in the Confucian worldview and epistemology of the time.[5]

The same can be said for Wang's discussion of Universal Principle, which encourages scholars to reconsider connections between the various strands of thought in the late-Qing and Republican periods (especially the most radical and iconoclastic schools of thought) and debates from earlier times. Most importantly, this emphasis on the connections between Heavenly Principle and Universal Principle draws out different possibilities and connections as potential resources for the present day.

The final section, "China's Modern Identity and the Transformation of Empire," engages in a wide-ranging discussion of how events in modern Chinese history relate to the idea of China as a modern nation-state and to frameworks for understanding nationalism and state building in the modern period. Wang is keen to test well-known models of nationalism, such as Benedict Anderson's argument about the role of vernacular languages and print-capitalism in forming "imagined communities," against the history of the Qing, the Republic, and the People's Republic. In the case of the model of "vernacularization," Wang suggests that the leveling of the terrain between speech and writing, which Anderson portrays as an essential step in realigning the public and their relationship to intellectual and political elites, simply does not fit the experience of twentieth-century China. Wang finds not a failure of development but a case in which valuable historical resources for imagining Chinese identity were retained and used to new ends.

In the final pages, Wang returns to the idea of economic empire under globalization. As with his treatment of the nineteenth-century notion of empire, Wang cautions against imprecise uses of this term. Furthermore, he argues that a greater understanding of the transformations of state organization and sovereignty in the nineteenth and twentieth centuries may provide a path forward from the present moment. Thus Wang anticipates the closing line of *The Rise of Modern Chinese Thought*, which argues that "the history that modernity loftily and even proudly rejects contains the inspiration and possibilities for overcoming its crisis."[6]

One question that looms large in the complete version of *The Rise of Modern Chinese Thought* but does not receive extensive treatment in the present text is the critique of science and scientism in Chinese thought, society, and politics. Earlier versions of Wang Hui's efforts to address these questions—some of which are reworked in *The Rise of Modern Chinese Thought*—are available in English and, barring a complete translation of Wang's four-volume work, would make useful supplements to the present translation.[7]

*   *   *

In its original language, *China from Empire to Nation-State* engages with and inhabits the fraught territory of translation, mistranslation, and creative appropriation. To bring the work into English, the translator must make intelligible an astonishing array of texts from Chinese history, philosophy, and literature, while conveying Wang Hui's self-reflexive engagement with Chinese, Japanese, North American, and Western European scholarship on China and modern world history.

A few words are in order, then, about choices I made as a translator. The first and most important problem of translation lies in the conceptual pair of *tianli* and *gongli,* translated in this work as "Heavenly Principle" and "Universal Principle." The first character in the term "Heavenly Principle," *tian,* refers not only to "heaven" but to nature, the natural order, and, when elaborated in neo-Confucian thought, the moral order that links human beings to the cosmos. *Gongli,* translated in this work as "Universal Principle," held and continues to hold many possibilities for meaning in twentieth- and twenty-first-century thought. Generally speaking, it refers to a worldview that claims roots in the exact sciences—which are frequently marked as modern and Western—and that rejects the purportedly metaphysical or mystical aspects of Heavenly Principle. Although the astronomical or celestial resonances shared in English by the words "Heavenly" and "Universal" might dull the contrast we find between these terms in Chinese, the "universal" of Universal Principle still captures several aspects of *gongli* in both its historical usage and its application as an analytical category by Wang Hui. (Alternate translations for *gongli* are "public principle," "axiomatic principle," or "self-evident principle.") The resonance between "heaven" in Heavenly Principle and "universe" in Universal Principle also conveys a sense of the residual linkages between *tianli* and *gongli* that, Wang Hui emphasizes, were often disavowed in the moment of the emergence of *gongli* and its deployment as a master term. As Wang points out, Yan Fu's translation of Thomas Huxley's *Evolution and Ethics,* a watershed text in modern Chinese intellectual history, referred to evolution as "the transformations of Heaven" *(tianyan);* subsequent thinkers regularly referred to *tianyan*/evolution as one of the *gongli*/universal principles that governed the natural world and human life.

The process of translation also reveals the fluidity of fundamental terms such as "nation," "state," and "nation-state." Previous discussions of *The Rise of Modern Chinese Thought* have usually rendered Wang Hui's phrase *diguo/guojia eryuanlun* as "the empire/nation-state binary," taking the term *guojia* as equivalent to "nation-state." In other places, however, the term *guojia* must be rendered differently, with attention to the changes in this term as a conceptual category. In the late nineteenth and early twentieth century—precisely the time when "Universal Principle" eclipsed "Heavenly Principle" as a dominant way of ordering Chinese thought—the term *guojia* came to refer to the modern state as the institution that was, according to Peter Zarrow, "the primary focus of political concern and the locus of 'sovereignty.'"[8] The seminal translation of Hegel's *Philosophy of History* into Chinese completed by Wang Zaoshi (1903–1971) illustrates the complex movement of these concepts into Chinese. Wang's translation, after all, was a translation not of Hegel's German, but of the English translation of Hegel's text completed by John Sibree in 1857. In Wang Zaoshi's translation, we see the all-important category of "the State" rendered as *guojia*.[9] This slippage in the meaning of the Chinese term—much as "nation" comes to mean both ethnonation and the nation-state in common usage in English—provides a certain flexibility in Wang Hui's arguments. (In a number of places Wang also uses the term *minzu-guojia*, which translates more directly as "nation-state.") Greater clarity, however, is required in the English translation, so a close comparison will show that *guojia* is rendered as either "the state" or "nation-state," as appropriate.

Wang Hui's prose—especially in *The Rise of Modern Chinese Thought*—has a reputation for being difficult and unaccommodating to nonspecialists.[10] Complaints about difficulty echo concerns about "Europeanized" writing that have haunted Chinese prose since the institutionalization of language reforms in the first decades of the twentieth century. As a historian of literature and culture, I see Wang Hui's particular style as a product of the intellectual environment between 1990 and 2010, when, following the traumas experienced during the Great Proletarian Cultural Revolution and the Tian'anmen Incident, many intellectuals sought to create new spaces for imagining their relationship to the broader "public" and to the sweep of intellectual and cultural history. Wang's turn away from some of the stylistic conventions of Sinophone academic writing, which often prizes elegance and rhetorical flair, illustrates how difficult writing can provide a space for imagining new possibilities in thought, ethics, and language itself.[11] Prettifying Wang's prose for Anglophone readers, then, would dilute the intensity of his inquiry and obscure the historical context of his work. One stylistic choice that diverts from the Chinese text was to leave untranslated the repeated use of the classifier *yizhong* ("a type of" or "a kind of"), which, if reproduced mechanically in the translation every time it occurs in Chinese, would make many of Wang's arguments sound far more tentative in English than they read in the original.

Other aspects of the translation are standard for an academic work of this scope. Where possible, all long quotations from Chinese were matched to existing English translations; where the text quotes from a text that has been translated into Chinese, such as Hegel's *Philosophy of History*, a quotation from a published English translation is provided, with the note changed to reflect the new reference. Translator's notes are provided only to elaborate on specific terminology or references that might not be familiar to specialist readers, or to show other sources from which I have borrowed in preparing this translation. Because this text was intended as an overview to a four-volume work, it frequently directs readers to chapters found in the larger work. These directions have been moved from the main text to the endnotes.

I thank Gao Gengsong, Keith Quigley, and Joseph Durant for valuable research assistance in preparing the manuscript. Robert Green corrected more than his share of errors as I completed the final version of the text for publication. Wu Shengqing made many useful suggestions for translations of passages from classical Chinese. As always, Ted Huters provided advice and encouragement with this project. As I revised the translation, I also referred to a partial draft translation that had been prepared by Ted Huters. Wang Hui graciously answered many queries and provided guidance on translating key passages. I am also grateful to an anonymous reviewer for Harvard University Press, who read the manuscript very closely against the original and offered a number of suggestions for improvement. Any errors or omissions in the translation remain my responsibility.

China from Empire to Nation-State

Any effort to research history that strays too far from specific linguistic contexts and written texts in order to reduce a problem to a simple conclusion is bound to sacrifice too much historical sensibility. This introduction thus does not offer a thoroughgoing discussion of all of the contents of *The Rise of Modern Chinese Thought*, but rather draws out some theoretical issues that emerge from the process of the analysis of history and provides them to the reader as a reference for reading the entire book. My discussion focuses on two self-reflexive questions: First, what meanings are contained in the term "China" (especially "modern" China)? I am not referring to a history of the concept of "China,"[1] but an attempt to answer the following questions: What is the nature of the historical emergence or construction of modern Chinese identity, ideas of geography, and senses of sovereignty? No discussion of modern Chinese thought can avoid such a historical understanding of "China" (*Zhongguo*). Second, how do we understand China's "modern" (*Zhongguode xiandai*)? The concept of the "modern" is of course a term of self-affirmation used by modern people, a way for modern people to differentiate themselves from the ancients and their world. "Modern," then, is a differentiating concept—a way of dividing history into different eras and forms. What, then, is held in the transformations in thought to which this self-affirmation leads? Indeed, what forms the basis of this modern identity? Or, what exactly are the conditions that make it possible to draw dividing lines in history? No discussion of modern Chinese thought can avoid this self-understanding of the "modern." These two questions can be discussed through many different fields and approaches. The analysis in this book approaches these questions from a limited perspective—the perspective of intellectual history. I discuss the first question through an analysis of historical narratives about China, and begin an analysis of the second question by exploring the interaction between the worldviews of Heavenly Principle *(tianli)* and Universal Principle *(gongli)*.

ONE

Two Narratives of China and Their Derivative Forms

Whether explicitly or implicitly, all historical descriptions and analyses concerning China contain two types of narratives about China: a narrative of China as empire, and a narrative of China as nation-state. These two narratives are entangled with a variety of research models often put forward in China studies, including "stimulus and response," "tradition and modernity," "imperialism," and orientations toward local history. These narratives themselves, however, have not gained nearly enough attention in their own right because, to a certain degree, concepts such as "China," the "Chinese empire," and the nation-state have already come to be extremely "natural" categories that no longer require special definition. Essential questions remain, however: whether or not China really is an empire or a nation-state, how to understand Chinese identity in and of itself, and how to determine the relationship between China and modernity. In the narrative of China as empire, China is described as a nonmodern, despotic (antidemocratic) political form; as an agrarian (nonurban, noncommercial, and nonindustrial) ecology of production spread out over a vast geographical space; as a multiethnic "imagined community" or "civilization" that relies on cultural identity and identification (and not national and political identity); and as a world system or landmass that sees itself as at the center of a tribute system (and not subject to formal equality or a treaty system). These traits have defined not only the differences between the Chinese empire and early modern European nations and other cultures, but also

3

the vast gulf between China and modernity itself. In contrast, the narrative of China as nation-state holds that, since at least the beginning of the Northern Song dynasty, China already contained a model for national identity, commercial economic relations, a prosperous and diverse urban culture, a highly developed system of administration, a model for social mobility that extended across all social classes, a vibrant popular culture, an extremely long tradition of science and technology accompanied by a secular Confucian worldview, and a form for international relations that spanned great distances. In investigations and descriptions that emphasize these historical phenomena, China provided a model for modernity at the same level as that of early modern Europe. These two narratives, then, stand in opposition to one another even as they complement one another and, working at different angles, transform into other, more subtle, narratives.

The opposition between the empire narrative and the nation-state narrative is a derivative product of narratives of European nationalism; this opposition is also an important theme in nineteenth- and twentieth-century European theories of politics and economics. In the next section I will provide a more detailed analysis of these issues. First, however, I will discuss how these two narratives of China appear in various ways in China studies. Most readers will be familiar with a historical narrative shared by Chinese Marxist scholars and John K. Fairbank's "stimulus–response" model. In these narratives, researchers working from various perspectives interpret the changes that began with the Opium Wars as a historical process in which the Chinese empire transforms into a nation-state (i.e., the transformation of traditional society to modern society), thus placing the relationship between empire and nation-state into a temporal order. The combination of elements such as arguments about historical evolution based on the transformation of modes of production, imperialism, and theories of national self-determination form the better part of the framework of historical narratives provided by Marxist-Leninist scholars. Within this framework, Marxist scholars condemn various aspects of European nationalism and imperialism, including political domination, military encroachment, economic exploitation, and the capitalist division of labor on a global scale. At the same time, however, these scholars also see capitalism's eradication of traditional values and social relations as a necessary process of historical development and a universal model for development found in all human history. Marxists link the achievements of modernity (national independence, industrialization, and popular sovereignty) with colonized peoples' awakening, struggle, self-liberation, and labor-centered practices of daily life (including advances in technology and development of knowledge based on improvements in the methods of production), applying a historical dialectic in which resistance against external encroachment and struggles against internal oppression become a process in which historical agency is generated. Marxist scholars treat the relationship between East and West as a historical relationship between colonizer and colonized, but focus their narrative not on the West but on capitalism as a distinct phase of a universal history. At the same time, they work to uncover the sprouts of capitalism within Chinese history.[1] Within the framework of class analysis, Marxists use the categories of autocracy and the small-scale peasant economy to interpret large-scale unified governance and internal colonialism, confirming the existence of elements of capitalism internal to Chinese society. Diverging from Marxist frameworks of transformation of modes of production and class analysis, John K. Fairbank's "stimulus–response" model (and "hinterland–littoral" and other models), Max Weber's analyses of Confucianism, and Joseph R. Levenson's sketches from intellectual history on the conflict between history, values, sentiment, and rationality all tend to see China as a relatively self-contained civilization with distinct culture, values, and institutions. According to this line of argument, because of the lack of internal forces for capitalism, the process of modernization for Chinese civilization—no matter how exquisite or beautiful it might have been—began within a discourse that emerged from its confrontation with European civilization.[2] According to the logic of these "theories of civilizational difference" or "culturalism" that developed in Europe in the eighteenth and nineteenth centuries, Western modernity and Chinese civilization stand in a certain kind of tension with and opposition to one another, and it is only by changing Chinese tradition that it will be possible to bring China into the modern world. These modes of analysis, then, can all be classified in terms of an opposition between tradition and modernity. For example, Fairbank's discussion of the predicament faced by China in the late Qing makes a strong distinction between cultural nationalism and political nationalism. On the one hand, so-called cultural nationalism emerges from the political relations of a diverse empire, where the empire must appeal to a universal culture to serve as a basis for identity in a diverse society. On the other hand, so-called political nationalism is the product of the nation-state and capitalism. It demands that political national identity serve as a condition for the legitimacy of the nation-state; only the latter type of nationalism can form the basis for the modern sovereign state and its political culture (a culture of citizenship and a democratic system). These two historical narratives share some very obvious assumptions: traditional China (especially Qing-dynasty society) is seen as a Confucian, autocratic, agrarian society, marked by the prominence of the patriarchal clan system and the tribute system, unable to produce the political culture, social institutions, modes of production, and diplomatic/trade relations that drove the development of early modern capitalism. Modern China, therefore, was produced by the challenges presented by European capitalism, imperialism, colonialism, or modernity, and Chinese society was produced by responses to these stimuli. For both schools of thought, the Opium Wars symbolize China's painful encounter with the challenge presented by Western civilization and serve as a milestone in the birth of Chinese modernity.

With the expansion of Europe and its political-economic system in the nineteenth and twentieth centuries, the gentry, intellectuals, and political figures in China and other Asian countries launched self-strengthening movements modeled on the West while they continuously sought out sources of identity from within their own society. This transformation also gave rise to efforts to find modernity within China (or Asian societies). In the early twentieth century, for example, some intellectuals attempted to break down the East (China)/West binary to create a set of narratives about Chinese or Asian modernity that were independent from narratives of Western modernity. *Eastern and Western Cultures and their Philosophies (Zhongxi wenhua ji qi zhexue)* by Liang Shuming (1893–1928), which laid out a model for the evolution of Western, Chinese, and Indian societies, is one example of how European ideas of modernity (such as the concept of historical evolution) and the discourse on civilizational differences might be combined into a new narrative of world history.[3] This trend was not unidirectional, however: amid the tides of national liberation, Western intellectuals who were deeply troubled by Eurocentrism and the history of European colonialism began to rethink their standards about history and worked to change Eurocentric narratives of "world history." In this sense, the call to "discover history in China" is the product of a two-tiered process: on one level, it is a theme and direction continuously pushed forward by the process of Chinese intellectuals and historians from other Asian countries working to establish their own identity and agency. On another level, it is also the product of Western scholars' (especially the Fairbank school's) self-criticism. For these reasons, a book on the topic of "discovering history in China" won the sympathy and praise of a great many Chinese scholars as soon as it was translated into Chinese.[4] In the field of historical studies, however, efforts to "discover history in China" had already taken on substantial force and complexity well before the self-criticisms of the Fairbank school emerged in the 1970s. From 1894 on, Japan defeated China's navy and the forces of the eastward-expanding Czarist Russian Empire, beginning the expansion of its sphere of influence to continental East Asia and to Southeast Asia. As Japan fought with major Western powers for control of the Pacific, Southeast Asia, and continental East Asia, the creation of a new framework for world history and strategic perspective became an important direction in Japanese fields of knowledge. The Kyoto School, represented by outstanding historians such as Naitō Konan (1866–1934) and Miyazaki Ichisada (1901–1995), opened a unique field of research on the history of East Asia. They constructed a Sinocentric East Asian region as a historical universe that contained unique dynamics of and trajectories toward modernity. Naitō's famous thesis about the "Tang-Song transformation" argued that the Tang and Song periods underwent massive changes that involved the collapse of the system of hereditary aristocracy. This turn of events marked the beginning of a new era for the history of China and East Asia.[5] Working along the lines of this argument, a number of scholars have conducted detailed investigations and broad, synthetic analyses to discover a number of social and cultural characteristics of an "East Asian modern age": the dissolution of the system of hereditary aristocracy and the formation of a folk culture (including the rural landlord system); the development of long-distance trade and the formation of an awareness of the existence of multiple nationalities, two developments with world-historical significance; a state structure buttressed by the power of the imperial throne, a well-developed bureaucratic system, and a new military system; the rise of urban economies and cultures; and the development of a secular Confucianism and "national ideology" that complemented the aforementioned developments.[6] The Song dynasty is seen as a model Chinese dynasty, an early nation-state defined by a clear sense of national identity, a "more Chinese" (that is, more Confucian) China. These elements are used to create a framework that defines Song politics in terms of a state organized around a system of centralized administration (*junxian zhidu*) or an early nation-state that is markedly different than the Han- and Tang-dynasty imperial models (as well as the models of the Yuan and Qing). In the temporal framework of "antiquity–middle ages–early modern," a narrative of a modern age in "East Asia" is thus established, centered on the Song dynasty in the tenth century, fourteenth-century Korea, and seventeenth-century Tokugawa Japan. The category of "East Asia," characterized by Confucian culture and the early nation-state, is expansive enough to include China, the Korean peninsula, and other regions. According to this narrative, the "East Asian modern age" is independent from the historical phenomena of the early modern West and occurs parallel to, if not sooner than, the process of modernization in Europe. This hypothesis of an "East Asian modern age" is a product of competition with or resistance to Eurocentric "world history." Even in new narratives of world history from contemporary times, we can still see derivative forms of this narrative: in narratives of Asian capitalism based on a framework of a tribute system with China at the center;[7] in narratives of the capitalist world system that focus on fourteenth- to eighteenth-century China and its silver-based economy;[8] and in notions of "Asia" that developed from a combination of the two preceding narratives. All three of these narratives may be seen as further developments of the "East Asian modern age" thesis.

At its core, the Kyoto School's narrative of East Asian modernity was established within a framework that competed with Western modernity. For the express purpose of overturning and breaking up European frameworks of "world history," the Kyoto School used an analysis of "nationalism" to argue that the tenth and eleventh centuries marked the beginning of early modernity in East Asia. Combining a strategic worldview with deep historical insight, these imperial historians created a "history of East Asia" within a new framework for world history. This attempt to overturn Western narratives of modernity, however, was simply an Asian version of those narratives because within this new narrative, the empire/ nation-state binary established by nineteenth-century European political economy still occupies the position of "metahistory." In scholarship produced by the Kyoto School, the concept of East Asia is not merely a geographical concept; it also includes a way of understanding social forms, political institutions, cultural identity, and relations between ethnic and national groups, as well as a method for placing this understanding into a temporal framework of antiquity–middle ages–early modern. This concept of East Asia, therefore, contained an experiment that attempted to perform parallel comparisons and differentiations by applying criteria of what constituted modernity against varying historical and geographical conditions—that is, an experiment to combine the categories of East Asia and modernity. These methodological issues are very clearly present in the writings of Naitō and Miyazaki. Whether in terms of criteria or chronology, their definition of "East Asia" is extremely similar to that of the concept of "the West" defined in histories of early modern Europe. In this respect, it is useful to compare their concept of East Asia with the formation of ideas about the early modern West. Harold J. Berman has analyzed the relationship between the concept of the West and modernity as follows:

> As a historical culture, a civilization, the West is to be distinguished not only from the East but also from "pre-Western" cultures to which it "returned" in various periods of "renaissance." . . . The West, from this perspective, is not Greece and Rome and Israel but the peoples of Western Europe *turning* to the Greek and Roman and Hebrew texts for inspiration, and *transforming* those texts in ways that would have astonished their authors. Nor, of course, is Islam part of the West, although there were strong Arabic influences on Western philosophy and science, especially in the period with which this study is concerned.[9]

In his discourse of the "Western legal tradition," Berman links "the West" with "peoples of Western Europe"; these "peoples of Western Europe" refer to England, Hungary, Denmark, Sicily, and others in the eleventh and twelfth centuries (i.e., the High Middle Ages). Their conflict with the Roman Catholic Church resulted in new urban, secular legal systems grounded in the political rule of royal courts. During this period, countries faithful to the Eastern Orthodox Church such as Russia and Greece, as well as areas such as Muslim-controlled Spain, were largely excluded from "the West." As a legal historian, Berman draws a close relation between "the West" and the "modern" by focusing on "the West," the "nation," and "secular power" and its legal system—in other words, by focusing on the same historical factors that are directly related to the modern nation-states that later developed:

> Modern times—not only modern legal institutions and modern legal values but also the modern state, the modern church, modern philosophy, the modern university, modern literature, and much else that is modern—have their origin in the period 1050–1150 *and not before.*[10]

The Kyoto School uses a very similar framework to elaborate an "East Asian modern age": in this narrative, modern political, legal, and cultural traditions emerge when a politically unified, multinational empire gives rise to an early modern state (a state with a mature system of centralized administration), early modern religion (secular Confucianism), early modern philosophy (Song-dynasty neo-Confucianism [*lixue*, "studies of moral principles" or moral philosophy]), an early modern educational system (the civil service examination system), and many other developments. All of these systematic transformations are then placed on an evolutionary timeline. In chronological terms, according to the Kyoto School narrative, these developments are almost completely parallel with early modern Europe.

The empire/nation-state narrative framework has also produced a variety of supplementary narratives, but none have shaken the basic structure and criteria of judgment in this framework. Marxist scholarship, American economic-social history, and contemporary cultural studies have all focused on topics such as the sprouts of capitalism in the late Ming and the economy and urban culture of the Jiangnan region, arguing from various perspectives that the seventeenth century was a key period in which early modernity in China came to a premature end. Differences between their individual positions can often be traced to varying understandings of European modernity or the origins of capitalism. Working much in the same vein as the Kyoto School's discussions of the "capitalist" tendencies of Song-dynasty economy, politics, and culture, these narratives seek to uncover the forces of modernity held within Chinese history. Narratives of the "sprouts of capitalism" in the Ming and Qing dynasties contain an unspoken assumption: within Chinese society, there exists a path of capitalist development similar to that of Europe. The premature demise of this early modernity (early capitalism, an era of early maritime activity, early urban culture) can then be traced to the feudal nature of Chinese society, and especially to the external factors of the seventeenth-century Manchu invasion and subsequent establishment of the Qing dynasty. Even so, it has been argued that elements of these "sprouts of capitalism" in the economic domain and "enlightenment thought" (*qimeng sixiang*) in the cultural domain were not completely eliminated, but remained latent within China under Qing imperial rule and responded to external challenges in the eighteenth century and after.[11] Slightly different from these narratives is Weber's *Konfuzianismus und Taoismus:* according to his theoretical perspective, modernity and rationalization can be understood within the same category, while temporal factors gain significance only when they establish relations with this category. Originally the empire/nation-state binary was an antithesis between two political structures (discussed in more detail later in the next section). From the beginning, however, it was also related to the dualistic relation of East (Asia)–West. In this second layer of relationships, the problem of political structures is converted into a methodological question of culturalism or a discourse on civilizational differences in the study of history. Within a framework based on a discourse of civilizational differences, Weber places rationalization or rationalism in a central position in his general discussion of Chinese history. As criteria for surveying historical events, rationalization and rationalism are produced by Weber's understanding of the spirit of

European capitalism. This same yardstick, however, is implicitly applied in observations made about the histories and civilizations of China and India. In this major work of social theory and historiography, Weber argues that a type of "political rationalism" already existed during the pre-Qin era—mostly during the Zhou dynasty, which was established prior to the unifications brought about by the Qin and Han dynasties. This political rationalism, which was extremely similar to the rationalism of early modern Europe, was produced from the competition and rivalries between the states controlled by the feudal princes. In his comparisons of European, Chinese, and Indian religions and civilizations, Weber's main assertion is as follows: this political rationalism found in ancient China lacked an accompanying economic rationalism and eventually died out under the political structures of the Qin and Han empires, failing to produce the spirit of capitalism that ultimately could only be produced by the European Protestant ethic.[12] What this interpretation of pre-Qin "political rationalism" serves to support is a contrast between the framework of an empire unified under the Qin and Han and that of the competitive nation-state. According to this contrast, the unified empire and the institutions that support its internal operations—regardless of whether they are in China or in the West—hinder the establishment of political-economic conditions that give rise to modernity or capitalism. As I show in my discussion of "International Law of the Spring and Autumn Period" (*Chunqiu guoji gongfa*) in chapter 6 of the full book, Weber's views on China were closely related to nineteenth-century Western missionaries' descriptions of China. In order to convince Chinese people to operate according to international law, and in order to convince Europeans to expand the purview of international law beyond its previous boundaries of the Christian world to include the Asian region (and, within it, China), nineteenth-century European and American missionaries repeatedly demonstrated that a kind of rationalism similar to that found in European nation-states had existed in China and even argued that the earliest source of international law might be found in China. Identical to Weber's analysis of rationalism in Chinese antiquity, this "ancient Chinese international law" based on the *Spring and Autumn Annals (Chunqiu)* and the *Rites of Zhou (Zhou li)* saw its origins in the relations between feudatory states established under the Zhou dynasty's system of enfeoffment. The unified system of the Qin and Han, however, led to the total disappearance of this political rationalism and ancient international law. China of the late-Qing dynasty, then, had to retrieve this political tradition, lost for two millennia, through European international law. This account of political rationalism in the Western Zhou is established on a disavowal of political models seen since the Qin and Han dynasties; at its core, then, lies the empire/nation-state binary.

We find, then, two antithetical narratives. In one, the conflict between East and West in the era of the Opium Wars represents the beginning of China's modernization; in the other, "capitalism" in the Northern Song dynasty serves as the origins of early modernity in East Asia. Both narratives, however, are chiefly concerned with seeking out the origins of "modernity" or a "modern era" in China or East Asia. Somewhat differently, narratives of capitalism in the Ming and Qing dynasties or narratives of pre-Qin political rationalism have offered accounts of the existence of elements of modernity within Chinese history, but their ultimate concern is to provide evidence for why "elements of modernity" internal to Chinese history ultimately were unable to produce European-style capitalism or modernity—or, put another way, to answer the question of why modern capitalism could only occur in the West. In the former set of narratives, the truncation of late-Ming modernity or capitalism and the Manchu invasion and subsequent establishment of the Qing dynasty are matters of direct historical consequence. In the latter narratives, however, pre-Qin political rationalism that was produced by competition among feudatory states (a type of political model similar to European monarchies or nation-states) was snuffed out by the political unification achieved under the Qin and Han empires. It is very clear that all of the aforementioned narratives of modernity see the following as signs of modernity: the nation-state, urbanization, industrialization, and newly emergent ethical relations that can be distinguished from orthodox Confucianism. Despite their different perspectives and points of view, they all see the empire, the agrarian empire, or the unified empire (and the feudal social system within this empire) as the antithesis of modernity and very rarely discuss anything about the relationship between the concept of "empire" and traditional

Chinese political concepts such as "enfeoffment" *(fengjian)* and centralized administration *(junxian)*.[13] According to the standards assumed by the Kyoto School, both Song- and Ming-dynasty "capitalism" were produced in a political-economic structure ruled by a relatively homogenous ethnic-Han dynasty, while in Weberian arguments about political rationalism, it was the unified, multiethnic imperial system that acted as a thoroughly stifling political structure. Within the aforementioned frameworks, the unified system of the Qin and Han dynasties stifled the competition-oriented political rationalism of the Zhou dynasty; the Mongol Yuan dynasty cut short the capitalism of the Song dynasty; and the Manchu invasion annihilated both the Ming dynasty's sprouts of capitalism and an individualistic culture developing in urban areas. Even if various sprouts of capitalism or modernity existed within Qing-dynasty society, the empire and its social system still formed a mechanism for stifling and preventing the emergence of modernity. Based on some of the key points of the previously described narratives, some more radical and daring scholars have evaluated China using the criteria of "state *(guojia)*" and "nation *(minzu)*," concluding that "China *(Zhongguo)*" is not a true modern state, but an empire; that "China" does not possess a national people with an internally consistent identity, but rather is a social entity yoked together by the force of its elite culture, lacking internal connections and the identity of a single social entity. Behind these two premises lies a more fundamental premise (of which authors are often not entirely conscious): the existence of a "state" *(guojia)* and a "nation" *(minzu)* are the basic conditions for adapting to capitalism and for the formation of democratic systems.[14]

However, regardless of whether one takes the expansion of Europe into Asia as the beginning of Chinese modernity or sees the Song dynasty or Ming dynasty as the starting point for early modernity, it is difficult to overcome the problem of how to explain the very prominent and direct historical relationships between the Qing dynasty and modern China. If one simply treats the Qing dynasty as the antithesis of modernity, then how can we explain the relationships between modern China and the Qing in such areas as demographic composition, territorial borders, cultural identity, and political structure? Can one really argue that the "modern" can override these types of specific and far-reaching historical relationships and structure and establish itself independently? Historians have made a number of important efforts to overcome the internal tensions and obvious deficiencies found in the aforementioned narratives of modernity. The first type of interpretation combines the historiographical teleology found in the discourse of "antiquity–middle ages–early modernity" with a cyclical view of dynastic rule in China. By focusing on the development of bourgeois society or a "modern transformation" of the *Lebenswelt* (lifeworld), this first type of interpretation places the Song, Yuan, Ming, and Qing dynasties in the category of "modern," downplaying the differences between the unified, Han-ethnic Song and Ming dynasties and the multiethnic empires of the Yuan and Qing dynasties. For example, in his explanation of why the Yuan dynasty did not issue a new legal code, Miyazaki Ichisada refused to make an argument based on the differences between nomadic empires and the dynasties of China proper, arguing instead that social changes taking place since the Song dynasty led to a situation where it was impossible to maintain and follow the traditional legal system, and thus the Yuan dynasty's decision not to promulgate a new legal code could only prove the continuity in social life between the Song and Yuan. Miyazaki's argument tries to describe "East Asian modernity" by incorporating a cyclical model of "Chinese dynasties" and a framework for the evolution of social life in the early modern period. This strategy makes a unique combination of two types of temporal models: on the one hand, a model of cyclical dynastic change and the continuous evolution of social life and, on the other hand, the model of antiquity–middle ages–early modern.[15] The most convincing part of this argument lies in the way it demonstrates that the Mongol and Manchu invasions did not result in the destruction of elements of modernity that had been developing since the Song dynasty, but, in fact, the opposite: foreign invasions could *not* alter the course of transformations that were already occurring in daily life, which only confirms the coherence of the "East Asian modern age" thesis. The second type of interpretation seeks out internal developments within Qing dynasty society, moving from large-scale accounts of the Qing dynasty to particular local historical changes, treating these local changes as internal forces leading to the disintegration of the dynasty and the transformation of Chinese society. For example, in the field of social history, research by Philip Kuhn has examined the challenges and destruction wrought by the Taiping Heavenly Kingdom movement on a Qing dynasty society buttressed by imperial and gentry power. Kuhn discovered that this historical movement led to monumental transformations in the gentry class and its functions, concluding that the destruction of the Qing dynasty and the process of the disintegration of traditional social structures were identical. The conclusion drawn from this account is that the end of the Qing dynasty and the beginning of modernity has some type of internal relationship.[16] In the fields of intellectual history and cultural history, various thinkers have drawn from the history of the Qing dynasty in the seventeenth through the nineteenth centuries to unearth traces of early enlightenment thought beginning in the late-Ming dynasty, as well as significant elements of scientific methods contained within Qing dynasty scholarship, thus providing an internal historical lineage for the transformation of thought and knowledge that took place in the nineteenth and twentieth centuries. This internal historical lineage can be seen as self-deconstructing elements contained within the authoritarian imperial system of the Qing dynasty, or may also be interpreted as a historical precondition for China's scholar-elite to accept new Western knowledge in the years following the Opium Wars.[17] A third interpretation is produced by a sense of suspicion toward democracy and the nation-state system and a rediscovery of cultural pluralism within the imperial system. According to this interpretive framework, the Qing dynasty should no longer be seen simply as a despotic, reactionary dynasty marked by racial violence, but as a multipolar empire capable of containing multiple institutions, laws, cultures, and religions. Research on the identities, customs, cultures, and legal systems of Manchu, Mongolian, Uighur, Tibetan, and various southeastern ethnic minorities have formed the bulk of the work on this narrative of a multipolar empire.[18] The new directions just described may in some ways be seen as a distant reply to the work of Owen Lattimore, who half a century ago undertook research on historical interactions between China and Inner Asia in the areas around the Great Wall.[19] The difference, however, is that Lattimore emphasized the deep relationships between agrarian and nomad societies on both sides of the

Great Wall, whereas contemporary research takes problems of ethnic identity and multipolarity as its starting point, offering narratives of empire that focus on multiple identities, multiple centers of power, diversity of laws, and multiple institutional frameworks, as well as the complex interactions between the patriarchal clan system and the gentry's emphasis on local government and reverence for feudal values. Taken together, this interpretation organizes its historical narratives around core categories and criteria such as multipolarity, decentralization, and self-governance of society.[20] This account of a multipolar empire begins within a framework that reflects on the nature of nationalism, and is directed against the modern sovereign state and its legitimacy: the sovereign state is predicated on the expropriation of the multipolar empire, and thus the modern state is characterized not by political democracy, industrial development, and individual freedom, but rather by internal colonialism, cultural homogeneity, and the autocracy of the unified, central state.

Narratives of empire established within frameworks of multipolar power, decentralization of power, and localism are becoming a new trend, but because narratives of multipolarity take ethnic identity, geographical relations, and political structure as basic narrative units, some mutual communication exists between research on the internal multipolarity of empire and narratives predicated on national self-determination, resulting in a situation in which narratives of empire are frequently dominated by the national narrative. In fact, in order to critique orthodox narratives of the state, narratives of multipolarity frequently make use of narratives of (minority) ethnicity to resist the national narrative. This tendency can already be seen in the work of Lattimore and Joseph F. Fletcher on Mongolia, the Hui regions of China, and Tibet. (They generally sympathized with national self-determination movements.) Contemporary research also continues to echo their work.[21] For example, research on the uniqueness of Manchu identity within the Qing empire served as a historical precedent for narratives of Manchuria and Manchukuo;[22] research on the Dzungars and their role in the war between Russia and the Qing dynasty has provided a well-rounded portrait of the Dzungar state, including political structures, demographic formations, geographical regions (borders), and national culture;[23] research on Hui, Miao, and other ethnic groups in

Yunnan, Guizhou, Taiwan, and southeastern China has taken shape within a framework of "Chinese colonialism."[24] Manchu, Mongolian, Tibetan, or other southeastern minority groups all possess their own unique identity, and, at various times, had their own political structures (different regional identities also existed in Han ethnic areas), but what kinds of relationships exist between these different identities? Moreover, what is their relationship to "Chinese identity"? These questions relate to the problem of how to understand the conditions for diverse identities within the dynasty's models of legitimacy; they also involve the question about whether or not the possibility exists to describe China in a way that moves beyond the nation-state narrative model. (For example, Chen Yinke argued that the Sui and Tang dynasties could be understood as part of the long-term interactions between China proper and various peoples of the northern frontier, thus revealing the fundamental hybridity of the "Chinese system." When seen in this light, Chinese identity itself must also be discussed in terms of conditions of interaction.)

At this point it is necessary to perform an analysis of questions of "Chinese colonialism" and "Qing imperialism" that appear in contemporary scholarship on China. The concept of "Chinese colonialism" relies on the following two premises: first, an affirmation of the narrative of the cyclical nature of Chinese dynasties and of the continuity between the Manchu Qing dynasty and modern China (i.e., seeing the Manchu Qing expansion into neighboring territories as part of the category of "Chinese colonialism" or "Chinese expansionism," which undoubtedly requires first affirming that the Qing had occupied an orthodox, legitimate position among Chinese imperial dynasties); second, a point of view that sees the southwestern border regions as external to the political unit of China. In these accounts of the Qing, complex historical relationships between such categories as "Manchu empire," "Han ethnicity," "China," and "non-Han minority ethnic groups" are not analyzed, and the concept of "Chinese colonialism" becomes a source of confusion in historical accounts. First, the legitimacy of the Qing dynasty as a Chinese dynasty was only established as the Qing gradually took control of China proper. For a substantial period of time after the Manchus' entry into China proper, Han people and southeastern ethnic minorities living in China proper as well as neighboring states did not recognize the Manchu Qing as a Chinese dynasty. For this reason, in the history of the Qing dynasty, we are constantly questioning the exact basis or historical time frame on which to distinguish between a Manchu dynasty and a Chinese dynasty. In other words, we must answer the question of how to define the relationships between such categories as "Manchu" and "Chinese," "Han ethnic" and "Chinese," "Qing dynasty" and "China." Second, we might also ask what is the significance of the fact that, after the founding of the Qing dynasty, policies were implemented to seal off the regions in the northeast and northwest regions that are the historical homelands of the Manchus and Mongolians, but vast numbers of ethnic Han nonetheless immigrated to these regions in the eighteenth and nineteenth centuries, resulting in new kinds of ethnic relations. Should this phenomenon then be explained in terms of "Chinese colonialism," or should it be explained in terms of social mobility that resulted from the unification of geographical territory under the Qing court? Third, on the authority of the Ming-dynasty system that it inherited, the Qing dynasty authorized and encouraged Han people to immigrate to southeastern regions such as Yunnan and Guizhou, which resulted in large-scale conflicts with the Miao and Hui peoples and a series of major disasters. (For example, conflicts in Yunnan that took place in the 1870s resulted in a 90 percent decline in the local Hui population.) Was this result the product of "Chinese colonialism," "Han colonialism," or the product of the Qing imperial system and the processes of its transformation? In a certain sense, the confusion that results in the interpretive processes previously described can be attributed to three factors. First among these is the hybridity of the category of "empire," a concept that is historically formed, repeatedly changes, and is difficult to define accurately. Since the nineteenth century, this concept has achieved relative stability only when it has been used in accounts that place it in opposition to the nation-state or national self-determination. The second factor is the question of how to understand the category of "China" (Zhongguo), an ancient concept that only in the modern era has been used to refer directly to a country. Over a long period of historical time, the population, geography, and political communities referred to by this concept underwent continuous changes. Therefore, when discussing the concept of "Chinese colonialism" in Qing-dynasty society, the inevitable question becomes: What is, or was, "China"? The third factor relates to changes to the connotation and denotation of the concept of "colonialism." The concept of colonialism was produced through the process of Europe's discovery of the coast of southern Africa (1488) and the American continent (1492) and its expansion into those territories. From that time on, European maritime hegemony expended from the Mediterranean Sea toward the Atlantic Ocean. The emergence of nation-states such as Portugal, Spain, Holland, France, and England are closely related to this maritime expansion. When it is used to describe the expansion and dominance of these countries in the period from the sixteenth century through the nineteenth century, the concept of "colonialism" is intertwined with mercantilist capitalism and early industrial capitalism. But in contemporary discourse, the content of the category represented by the term "colonialism" has broadened to the point that it describes virtually all organized attempts at expansion (whether by empires, nations, or alliances of nations, etc.) undertaken with the goal of seizing economic and population resources from other areas; but this expanded definition does not necessarily take into account the historical relationship between colonialism and capitalism. As a result of this change, the exclusive use of this term to castigate Western hegemony, invasion, and exploitation is also changing.

Quite similar to the change in the concept of colonialism, the scope of application of the concept of imperialism has also expanded. Separate from a concept of empire that emphasizes cultural pluralism and general unity, the concept of imperialism focuses on the state and its expansionist policies; in this sense, it is based on the same logic as a concept of "Chinese colonialism" that stresses economic exploitation and ethnic conflict. Following the logic of Lattimore's description of grassland societies, one trend in contemporary research describes the Qing dynasty as an imperialist structure that continuously expands from the continental interior to the coastal regions. However, completely unlike Lattimore, who divided the expansion of powers from the Asian hinterlands into pre-Western and post-Western, agrarian/nomad and industrialized forces, this new concept of "Qing imperialism" no longer shows interest in the historical relationship between the category of imperialism and industrialization/capitalism. In this type of scholarship, Manchu, Mongolian, northwestern ethnic minorities, southeastern ethnic minorities, and Ming-dynasty China are all described as independent political entities or nation-states. The Manchu expansion and occupation of these areas, then, is described as a process of state-centered imperial expansion. The logic behind this description shows continuity with the Kyoto School's way of describing ethnic relations during the Five Dynasties period and the Song dynasty's relations with the various "states" (guo), which is to say that they all attempt to place "China" into a system of states that are formed through ethnic sensibilities, or to place "China" within a strict nation-state (or nation-state in a pre-nation-state era) framework. Concepts such as "Qing imperialism" or "Manchu imperialism" are produced through this logic. The concept of "Qing imperialism" has avoided some of the confusion that may have resulted from the concept of "Chinese colonialism" and its treatment of the Qing dynasty, the Manchus, and China, arguing that the Opium Wars were a conflict between two global hegemons represented by a continuously expanding Qing imperialism and by British imperialism.[25] This argument shares some similarities with nationalist narratives.[26] If this explanatory model is placed within the historical context of theories of imperialism, then we can see very clearly its internal continuity with the European tradition that describes the imperial expansions of ancient China, the ancient Near East, and Greece as imperialism, as well as a variety of responses to modern theories of imperialism. The narrative of "Qing imperialism" emerged against the backdrop of changes that occurred beginning in the 1980s in research in the Western scholarly world on colonialism; it also shares some connections with postcolonial theory, which is characterized by an emphasis on the interactions between colonizing states and their colonies.

In modern history, discussions about the causes behind and values of imperialism can generally be divided into four major discourses. Aside from apologist theories of imperialism that explain its origin in the need for national security and liberation from despotic government, there are two theories that, despite substantial differences between them, hold great explanatory power. The first theory is represented by Adam Smith, David Ricardo, J. A. Hobson,[27] and Marxist theorists such as Rudolf Hilferding,

Vladimir Lenin, N. I. Bukharin, Rosa Luxemburg, and Karl Kautsky. (To this group I would also add Karl Polanyi, author of *The Great Transformation*.) They discuss the forces of imperialism in terms of possession of economic resources (population, natural resources, and markets), using various means to draw connections between this expansionist national policy and capitalist economics. Imperialism, they argue, is closely linked to the capitalist mode of production and its crises: financial capital produced by the combination of industrial capital and capital held by banks, the expansion of capital flows, and increases in military production and militarist politics all serve as conditions for the production of imperialism. The main difference between Smith, Ricardo, and Hobson, on the one hand, and Lenin and Bukharin, on the other, is that the former group believes that imperialism is beneficial only to a small part of the nation and not the entire nation, whereas the latter group puts forward the idea of "ruling nations," arguing that imperialism is a late stage or the highest stage of capitalism.[28] The second theory is represented by Machiavelli, Sir Francis Bacon, Ludwig Gumplowicz, Adolf Hitler, and Benito Mussolini. From different standpoints, they argued that imperialism is rooted in the fundamental characteristics of groupings of human beings, i.e., that imperialism is a natural product of the battle for survival among groupings of human beings (especially states). In the latter half of the twentieth century, new changes in the historical landscape gradually gave rise to a method for observing phenomena related to imperialism over long periods of history that offered new ways to critique these classic models. For example, Giovanni Arrighi, influenced by the macrohistorical models of Ferdinand Braudel, contended that, contrary to arguments by Lenin and Hilferding that finance capital represents a particular stage of global capitalism, finance capital has in fact always been a distinguishing characteristic of capitalism.[29] In this sense, the concept of imperialism also cannot be limited to the nineteenth and twentieth centuries. Other scholars, even as they agree that imperialism was first a response to economic problems, have also emphasized cultural influences, especially cultural influences between colonizing countries and colonies. The long-term historical perspective has provided a kind of anti-Smithian framework and also critiques the empire/nation-state binary established by nineteenth-century political economy in two ways: first, it demolishes the judgments that classical liberalism makes about empires in its self-affirmation of modern society. Those judgments include the following: imperial control is fundamentally characterized by violence and, therefore, does not create favorable conditions for industrial production, and only modern society (the nation and civil society) is capable of relying on a system of production, circulation of commodities, and division of labor as described by Smith. Second, the long-term view establishes that imperial rule contained elements of capitalism, and that imperialism centered on the political structures of nation-states and their economic systems was heavily dependent on the use of violence. The differences between empire and imperialism, then, frequently were not nearly as great as had been previously imagined.

Be that as it may, the more recent historical accounts described earlier do not divert from the fundamental categories of capitalism and forms of capital in their discussion of the imperialism question. The concept of "Qing imperialism" has largely treated the question of imperialism within the scope of expansion of the state and competition for survival; these discussions have also touched on the conflict between forms of ritual practiced by the Qing court and the British Empire, but rarely focus on questions related to modes of production and economic forms. Any attempt to define the process of expansion of the Qing dynasty that began in the seventeenth century as imperialism clearly requires a departure from the scope of discussions of capitalism; in this respect, this narrative moves closer to the second type of theory of imperialism previously described. Therefore, the crux of the issue lies not in whether to affirm that expansion, expropriation, and colonization actually occurred during the Qing dynasty (of this there is no question), but whether to affirm that it is necessary to distinguish between similar phenomena that occur both under capitalism and noncapitalism—or between a traditional form of empire and the imperialism produced by the process of nineteenth- and twentieth-century European industrialization. The fundamental characteristics of modern imperialism and colonialism lie not only in military occupation, armed expropriation, and racial hierarchies, but also in a thoroughgoing transformation of the preexisting structure of the colonized society, as well as its subordination to the industrialization of the colonizing country's economic system, which, in turn, results in a type of global and unequal international division of labor. For this reason, a large number of studies of imperialism focus on such questions as development, accumulation, and dependency. Like other empires, the history of Chinese dynasties includes armed expropriation and ethnic domination. In certain places and times, these projects of expropriation resulted in the transformation of local social customs, habits, social structures, and systems of production (as in the remaking of the Dali kingdom during the Ming dynasty). Vast differences existed, however, in the workings of the so-called tribute system in different regions and areas: often the system was not at all interested in making changes to local customs and structures of production.[30] When seen from this perspective, various accounts of imperialism must also be related to the establishment of modern nation-state building and the forces behind it. At its core, the question remains: What exactly are the relationships between the political-military structure of the national state, the foreign policy of the sovereign state, and the reorganization of society that takes place under industrial capitalism?

Because traditional concepts of nationalism such as ethnicity, territory (borders), religion, and language continue to dominate narratives of social relations within an empire, it is impossible truly to break free from the binary relationship between empire and nation *(minzu)*. The narrative of "Qing imperialism" both omits any discussion of the historical relationships between imperialism and capitalism and largely ignores the differences between universal empire and competitive imperialisms rooted in nationalism.[31] Because the narratives of empire described earlier all contain internal and even more deep-seated elements of the nation-state narrative, it is quite natural to expect that these narratives of empire will be filtered through narratives of the nation-state or narratives of imperialism. In this filtering process, "imperialism," a concept that in English negotiates between empire and state, serves a unique function: it is a concept that binds the categories of empire and state. This combination, however, cannot cover up some of the historical distinctions between empire and nation-state: after the fall of the Roman Empire, the idea of empire as a unifying force was never again truly realized. The peoples that rose up from the ruins of the Roman Empire, Mongol Empire, and Islamic empires competed with one another in a fragmented environment, thereby producing a phenomenon that would later come to be known as imperialism. Therefore, even if imperialism shares the expansionist tendencies found in empires, from a global perspective, it is a divided and nonunified force that emerges between various nations *(minzu)* and states *(guojia)*, and is always closely related to state expansionist policies, practices, and propaganda related to the state's direct occupation of the territory and economic resources of other countries or other communities. It is for this reason, then, that narratives of "Qing imperialism" emphasize only the expansionist nature of the empire, but pay no attention to the distinctions between this model of expansion and so-called universal empires, and also rarely focus on important long-term transformations that occurred in the model of imperial rule of the Qing dynasty from the seventeenth to the nineteenth centuries. For example, how should we interpret the relationship between the tribute system of the early Qing, which was extremely flexible, and the expansion of the system of direct provincial rule that occurred in the latter part of the Qing?[32]

Narratives of empire, national narratives, and their derivative forms establish their views of China from a variety of perspectives. Can China be called a political entity with a continuous existence across the cycles of history? Is China an empire or a nation-state, or an empire merely passing itself off as a nation-state? Is "China" a political concept or a civilizational or cultural concept? How are we to understand Chinese nationalism and Chinese national identity? Amid theories of Orientalism and postcolonialism, concepts such as "interaction" *(hudong)*, "interconnectedness" *(xianghu lianjie)*, and "hybridity" *(hunzaxing)* have inspired peoples' imaginations, just as many other phenomena related to modernity have been gathered into blended categories, providing people with new ways of thinking about and describing a society and its identity. The concept of "entangled modernity" gives a powerful image to express the new ways used to imagine modernity; working with these new ways of imagining, some scholars have uncovered new models for understanding historical connections.[33] One result of viewing modernity in such terms as exchange, interaction, and hybridity is the denaturalization of the category of "China."

In other words, "China" as a natural and self-evident concept is destabilized, becoming an image of China that is hybrid and produced by historical interactions. If interaction and hybridity are characteristics of all cultures and societies, then does any internal consistency exist within the image of China that is created by interaction and hybridity? If we do not allow ourselves to be dazzled by contemporary scholarly rhetoric, then we see that these issues are in fact exactly the same as the questions that vexed major figures from the late-Qing period. We can see their basic forms in two models of nationalism from the late Qing: the Chinese (broadly defined) nationalism of Kang Youwei (1858–1927) and Liang Qichao (1873–1929), and the Han nationalism of Sun Yat-sen (1866–1925) and Zhang Taiyan (1868–1936). Kang Youwei and Chen Yinke (1890–1969) discussed such questions as "China," "Han ethnicity," and "Chinese culture" in terms of hybridity, attempting to use this view of a "hybrid China" to resist European-style ethnic nationalism and to form a capacious "Chinese identity" or imperial "Chinese identity."[34] In his dualistic rhetoric, working counter to Kang and Chen, Zhang Taiyan used the methods of evidential learning *(kaozhengxue)* to discover the sources of primordial Chinese *(Hua-Xia)* racial characteristics. Even if it was not without some degree of regret that he discovered the hybridity of the "Chinese race" *(Han zhong)*, he nonetheless insisted on a narrative of Han nationalism characterized by ethnicity.[35] If we say that, in the era of nationalism, the discovery of hybridity and interaction was nonetheless subsumed into various forms of nationalist narratives, then, within the discursive environment of contemporary globalization, when major intellectual currents use discussions of interaction and hybridity to deconstruct Eurocentrism and the nation-state, it must become unusually difficult to find any solid basis for the establishment of a collective identity in these narratives.

Within these historical processes, then, the question of how to understand "China" becomes extremely pressing. First, when compared with all other premodern empires, the scale and stability of the Chinese empire *(Zhonghua diguo)* are quite uncommon. In the words of Mark Elvin, "in the broadest of perspectives, the Chinese empire is the major exception in the premodern world to what would appear to be the rule that units of territorial and demographic extent comparable to that of China are not stable entities over long periods of time."[36] This "exception" is as follows: Over such a long period of time, how is the Chinese empire able to maintain the stability of its territory, population, and political unity? Second, the status of this "exception" is not limited to the "premodern world": in the twenty-first century, China is the only society in the world that, as a sovereign state and nation, has retained the territorial area, population, and political culture that it inherited from an empire that existed before the nineteenth century. Unlike other empires that underwent a process of fragmentation into sovereign states, nationalist and state-building movements in China in the late nineteenth and early twentieth centuries took the contents and characteristics of a composite universal empire system and brought them directly into the structure of the nation-state. Following the many armed conflicts and seizures of territory that occurred in the first half of the twentieth century, a massive, centralized bureaucratic system and its multilayered institutions (provinces, autonomous regions, and their subordinate institutions) that were rooted in the era of a unified empire was renewed through the revolutions of the modern period, forcefully organizing Chinese industry and agriculture into a complete, national economic system. From Sun Yat-sen's concept of "Five Races, One Republic" to Mao Zedong's call for a grand unification of the people of all ethnicities, a type of new Chinese national identity gradually began to take shape in a population of 94 percent Han ethnicity. Thus we ask the following questions: First, why did the Chinese revolution and state building not result in the type of disintegration that seems to have been unavoidable in other imperial structures? In other words, why was it possible for an imbricated historical relationship to emerge between the structure of Qing empire building and modern state building? Second, why were the Chinese revolution and process of state building able to successfully transform the property inherited from the empire into key aspects of revolution and development, thus producing a new kind of sovereignty out of the transformation of the fundamental form of the empire? Third, what exactly is the relationship between pre-nineteenth-century empire building and state building in the nineteenth and twentieth centuries? Concepts such as hybridity, the "imagined community," or constructedness have revised dualistic "China/West" narratives, providing help for understanding Chinese state building and processes in Chinese society within an endlessly rich and open network of relations. However, historical accounts of interaction, hybridity, and entanglement cannot forestall the following questions: If every nation is an "imagined community," then how did the resources that allow us to "imagine" China come into being? What is the relationship between the category of "China," on the one hand, and, on the other, the characteristics of an empire that recognizes diversity and difference, relativizes the boundaries between inner and outer, and pursues unity and universality? Within narratives of hybridity, what is the status of the possibility for and imagination of a Chinese identity? Fourth, as a type of mechanism for control that is founded on the dual preconditions of violence and culture, the empire maintained a position of tolerance toward varying ethnic cultures, religious faiths, legal systems, and political economy. By comparison, the nation-state demands a high degree of unity in areas such as the political system, legal system, language, and culture, to the extent that when the majority ethnic group places itself in a position as the representative of sovereignty, marginal ethnic groups and their cultures confront challenges and possibilities of disintegration that are far greater than those seen in the imperial era. Therefore, we must also ask: Can the problem of political autocracy be discussed only in terms of the "imperial tradition," or must it also come into consideration when discussing the nation-state system itself? Can accounts of internal cultural relations in the imperial era provide a critical perspective and program for democracy that can allow for difference? Fifth, if the imperial era saw foreign relations that were much richer and more complex than previously imagined, then what exactly is the relationship between the model for international relations from the imperial era and the model for international relations in modern China?

Contemporary European states are attempting to transform the logic that negotiates between democracy and nation into a logic that negotiates between democracy and a larger Europe. Put another way, they are attempting to use a kind of imperial or suprastate structure to form a new model for identity and conditions for legitimacy that are capable both of accommodating various national identities and of affirming cultural differences. It is with a view to the future that efforts are made to examine the transformation of the nation-state system in the nineteenth century, to reflect on this history that has been concealed by narratives of the nation-state, and to seek out historical possibilities from it. For example, in the dialectical relationship between universality and diversity held within the concept of empire, what is the relationship between the preservation of social customs, habits, and locality, and the inevitable violence and logic of control associated with any historical empire? Can we find in it sprouts or elements of a type of post-nation-state political form? Consideration of this problem must not be obscured by nostalgia for empire or overly idealistic attitudes or methods. From my perspective, whether we are looking at debates about the legitimacy of the nation-state or idealized accounts of pre-nineteenth-century empires, all are established on the binary between empire and nation-state. Therefore, when answering the foregoing questions, we must analyze the process by which the empire/nation-state binary was formed.

TWO

The Empire/Nation-State Binary and European "World History"

The empire/nation-state binary in China studies is rooted in the intellectual traditions of nineteenth- and twentieth-century Europe. In contrast to the idea of the nation-state, a product of the nineteenth century, the concept of "empire" can be traced back quite far into European history. In Western languages, the term "empire" evolved from the Latin term *imperium*, which refers to legitimate authority or dominion. As an analytical category, however, the concept of empire only takes on clear significance through the process of the formation of the concept of the nation-state. Thus "empire," although an ancient word, is in fact a modern concept closely related to problems of nationalism. In the Chinese language, *diguo* (usually translated as "empire") has not been a commonly used word. A search in the mammoth *Emperor's Four Treasuries (Siku quanshu)* yields only eighteen instances of the word being used (when it is not a case of the characters *di* ("lord" or "lord on high") and *guo* ("state" or "kingdom") appearing next to one another without being used as a single word). An analysis of these occurrences shows that the term had two meanings: first, it referred in geographical terms to the territory/area of China and to the state brought together under the emperor's rule. For example, the "Memorial Written to Congratulate the Emperor on His Ascent to the Throne Today," from *Collection of Writings by the Hermit of Hongqing* by Sun Di (1081–1169), reads:

Summoning the six dragons and ascending the throne, the ruler takes the royal seat. . . . I congratulate the emperor with great respect as His majesty . . . issues his imperial policies extending for a thousand years; he inherits the boundless lands that have submitted [to him]; he pacifies the emperor's realm *(diguo)* from the four directions; and he extends his power to those places already in good order.[1]

In another example, "A Preface Written at a Banquet in at the Home of Wu Shaofu of Jiangning," Wang Bo (649–676), speaking of the wars at the end of the Han dynasty, wrote:

Mt. Jiang lies to the south, the Yangzi flows to the north; Wu Zixu was employed by the throne, and the Wu kingdom prospered. Sun Quan's territory was contained, and the nine provinces [i.e., China proper] fell into disarray. The remaining ruins and the old land are the ten-thousand-*li* imperial city; the tiger's lair and the dragon's dominion [i.e., Nanjing] form the empire *(diguo)* that reigns for three hundred years.[2]

In "Rhyme-Prose with Preface on the North Star Tower *(Gong zhen lou),*" Chen Fei (fl. 2nd century C.E.) wrote: "This morning my thoughts were particularly far away, and thus I climbed the tower. To the south I can see my home town, and my eyes gaze out to the empire *(diguo)* in the north."[3] In "Preface to the Writings of Xuan Bangzhi Presented to Vice Magistrate Wang [Zihua] Upon Channeling the Yellow River," Zhang Guowei (1595–1645) wrote:

The river springs from the Kunlun Mountains; its waters flood the central lands *(Zhongguo),* and one cannot avoid the work of guiding and channeling it. Once the waters were brought under control, later generations enjoyed the benefits of this work, and the wealth of all taxes and tributes from near or far flowed from the river to the empire *(diguo).*[4]

Second, the notion of *diguo* is used to refer to the virtuous rule of the mythical Five Emperors. This argument originated in Wang Tong's maxim that the states ruled by a lord on high *(di)* "employ virtue to do battle" *(zhan de)*. In the *Doctrines of the Middle Way*, Wang is recorded as saying:

> The Master Wenzhong said: When the power of the king is exhausted, the feudal princes will rise up in the name of righteousness; when the rule of the lord on high *(di zhi)* falls into decline, all under heaven will speak of what is to their own advantage. Master Wenzhong said: states led by usurpers employ armies to do battle; they depend on force alone. States led by hegemons employ wisdom to do battle; subduing the armies of others without doing battle is accomplished by wisdom. States led by kings employ righteousness to do battle; keeping the people from doing wrong requires more than wisdom. States led by a lord on high *(diguo)* employ virtue *(de)* to do battle; those who are benevolent have no enemies under Heaven, and their virtue is known to all. States led by emperors *(huang)* employ nonaction *(wuwei)* to do battle.[5]

The Chan monk Qisong (1007–1072) wrote in an essay "Concerning Armies" *(Wen bing)*:

> The Master Wenzhong said: lost states employ armies to do battle; states led by hegemons employ wisdom to do battle; states led by kings employ benevolence and righteousness to do battle; states led by a lord on high *(diguo)* employ virtue *(de)* to do battle; and states led by emperors *(huang)* employ nonaction *(wuwei)* to do battle. Nothing can surpass a sage-king, who can act according to benevolence and righteousness. And thus it is said: benevolence and righteousness is all that is needed. The superior man does not involve himself with obscure arts of astrology or with disloyal, deceitful men who take up arms. How, then, could I involve myself in such matters?[6]

In the *Daily Jottings of Master Huang (Huangshi ri chao)*, Huang Zhen (1213–1280) wrote:

> How can we say that there was order in the earliest times? It was only in later times, when the Sage Kings were born, that order came to the world. Moreover, even if the ruler practices nonaction, how

can those below provide for themselves? It is said that states led by a lord on high (*diguo*) employ virtue (*de*) to do battle, and that states led by emperors (*huang*) employ nonaction (*wuwei*) to do battle. As for speaking of battle in terms of virtue and nonaction, although such discussions may use the words of Laozi, they are not necessarily in accord with the Way . . . Alas! [It is unfortunate that] Master Wen-zhong has been said to have spoken these words, and later generations may have manipulated his words to make people believe so.[7]

The preceding pieces of evidence show that we can grasp the meaning of *diguo* ("empire") on three levels. First, *diguo* exists alongside such concepts as enfeoffment (*fengjian*) and centralized administrative structure (*junxian*), all of which refer to a political community with specific values and forms. Second, *diguo* is a political form that is placed on a historical sequence that runs through the mythical Three Kings and Five Emperors of antiquity (*san huang wu di*), the Zhou kings, the hegemons of the Spring and Autumn period, and the contending powers of the Warring States period. That is, it represents a political form and ethical direction from the era of the Five Emperors that is characterized by "virtue" and distinguished from those states founded by usurpers, hegemons, and kings and their associated political forms. Third, the concept of *diguo* represents a disavowal of those political systems whose constant struggles for power resulted in an endless series of political plots and military conflict.

Obvious differences exist between this concept of *diguo*, which emerged from the states of the Five Emperors, and both the concept of empire from Western antiquity and the concept of empire that entered Asia in the nineteenth century: whereas the first usage of *diguo* is based on virtuous rule, the latter two are based on overarching, absolute imperial sovereignty and a form of power based on the unified state. In a certain sense, an "empire" that "employs virtue to do battle" is something that can only be conceived of in relation to political forms such as those that "employ armies to do battle" or "employ wisdom to do battle." The concept of empire that we are familiar with today, however, is a product of the nineteenth century. The Meiji emperor named his state the "Empire of Great Japan" (*Dai Nippon teikoku*) in 1868; following this event, this new concept of empire entered China in the late nineteenth century. This concept of empire was closely linked to the form of the absolutist state and militarist social systems—and therefore completely different from the concept of *diguo* ("empire") found in ancient Chinese texts. In a certain sense, the new concept of empire that took shape during the nineteenth century was actually closer to the political structures *repudiated* by the ancient concept of *diguo* (e.g., hegemonic states, dictatorial states), and might even be used to describe the emperors who gained power during the Qin and Han periods and the great unified states that were under their control (i.e., the monarchical system found under the system of imperial power and centralized administration). In pre-Qin documents, *di* (lord on high) or *shangdi* (sovereign on high) are other names for *tian* (Heaven), a concept that is characterized by moral character, dominance, and universality. When the first emperor of Qin (Qin Shi Huang) conquered the six rival kingdoms and established a unified state, he gave himself the title "First Emperor" *(Shi huang)* and used this moniker to distinguish himself from the titles given to the Zhou kings. In the fifth year of the Han dynasty (202 B.C.E), all under heaven *(tianxia)* was unified, and the feudal princes recognized the Han monarch as the emperor; this event also demonstrated that imperial power exceeded the universal political power that had been in place under the system of enfeoffment. At this time the concept of "emperor" (*di* or *huangdi*) was understood on three levels. First, it was differentiated from the concept of the (Zhou) king that had been established on the basis of the system of enfeoffment. The new idea of the emperor was established on a state system and centralized administrative structure *(junxian);* the imperial system, then, also involved the distinctions between the centralized administrative system *(junxian)* and the system of enfeoffment *(fengjian)*. Second, the emperor was also the Son of Heaven and was charged with carrying out the will of Heaven. The will of Heaven was carried out through the rites, music, and culture, and thus the emperor also represented cultural unity. Third, as the highest political power, the emperor also served as the lead commander of the military, with his personal leadership at the line of battle serving as the most important expression of imperial might and authority. In this sense, imperial authority and military conquest were closely related. It is important to note, however, that the European concept of "empire" was related to the Latin root of the term *emperor*. The emperor was first and foremost the supreme military commander; his role as symbol of imperial unity was secondary. For example, in Roman imperial discourse, the earliest usages of the term *emperor* referred to a successful general; only later was it used to refer to heads of state. Both the former and the latter usages have a strong military or martial connotation. When the Japanese emperor had overthrown the Tokugawa shogunate and established a unified, centralized state with its capital in Tokyo, he used the term "empire" (J: *teikoku,* Ch: *diguo*) to name his reign on the throne, a choice that showed the influence on his thinking of the British Empire and other European states and signaled that he was also appropriating the ancient categories of Heavenly Emperor and *diguo* from ancient Chinese thought. The combination of universal power and the unified state was achieved in part through the compound, synthetic term represented in Japanese by Sinitic characters: "帝国/*teikoku/diguo*/empire."[8]

In historical research on pre-nineteenth-century China, members of the Chinese gentry and Chinese scholars have always had misgivings about the concept of a "Chinese empire" so frequently applied by Western scholars. There are two sources for these misgivings. First, the majority of Chinese scholars do not agree that it is possible to discuss European empires and Chinese dynasties on the same terms, and argue that China and its world model largely depend on a model of assimilation through culture and ritual and "kingly transformation" *(wang hua),* through the virtue of the sovereign, of peoples from afar. According to this argument, China is different from empires based on military conquest such as the Roman Empire, Mongol Empire, or Ottoman Empire. Second, in a great number of its usages, the concept of empire has already been placed in a relationship of absolute opposition to the nation-state and even to modernity itself, and thus the designation of "empire" assumes in advance that Chinese society and culture is sealed off from the outside world, autocratic, and backward. Regarding the first point, many scholars who research the comparative history of empires have conceded that Chinese dynasties utilize Confucian scholars and the gentry class as a unique set of intermediaries, and that in the process of "kingly transformation," "culture" plays a far more powerful role than military conquest. This point, however, is not enough to refute or reject wholly the application of the concept of empire: Where, after all, in the histories of the Qin, Han, Sui, Tang, Song, Yuan, Ming, and Qing dynasties do we see a lack of historical records of military conquest? Among those European empires or Asian empires that are strongly characterized by military conquest (e.g., the Roman Empire, Ottoman Empire, Mughal Empire), how many did not use a universal "civilization" to structure its vision of the world and its own legitimacy? The real problem is not the application of the concept of empire, but how to break apart the empire/nation-state binary, and how, when conducting historical research, to manage appropriately the relationships between the concept of empire and other historical Chinese political concepts—enfeoffment (*fengjian*), "grand unification" (*da yitong*), centralized administrative system (*junxian*), tribute, and so on—as well as historical differences between the various Chinese dynasties. Naitō Konan and Miyazaki Ichisada argued that the Song dynasty could be understood as a centralized administrative state that was similar to the nation-state (in terms of group identity, a community with defined limits, bureaucratic systems, trade relations, civic culture, etc.), and thus could be distinguished from political communities represented by dynasties such as the Han, Tang, Yuan, and Qing, which all held extremely large territories, contained a multitude of ethnic groups, and were dominated by an aristocracy with unlimited power. Compared to the Song and Ming dynasties, the Qing dynasty's political structure, cultural ideology, and structures of ethnic groups all show a high degree of hybridity and limitlessness (this concept is understood relative to the clear boundaries of community established by the nation-state in terms of territorial borders and population). The Han, Tang, and Qing were all more similar to what is commonly understood as empire, and from the formation of their structures and institutions, we can describe some of their characteristics as follows: first, their hybrid systems and mechanisms of control are different from a pure system of enfeoffment (*fengjian*) or centralized administration structure (*junxian*). Second, they possess a society and economy of vast scope and a set of multinational ethnic relations that have been formed by military expansion, trade, and immigration. Third, they possess multiple structures of power, with concentrated central power and structures of power generated by local culture existing side by side. Fourth, they work to make their own culture universal or to serve as the representative of "civilization"; this type of universal culture or civilization, however, is characterized by its hybridity and is not monolithic. Following a groundswell of nationalism in the nineteenth century, the deep suspicion of this type of empire, with its multiple centers of power, multinational ethnic makeup, and limitlessness, came to serve as one historical justification for the legitimacy of the nation-state model. An unavoidable question remains, however: Since modern China was established on the historical foundations laid by the Qing dynasty, how are we to understand the continuities between "empire" *(diguo)* and "nation" *(minzu)*?

After his systematic inquiry into the meanings of the term "empire," Dominic Lieven concluded:

> Over the last two millennia the word "empire" has meant many different things to different people from different countries at different times. Indeed it has often had different meanings to people from the same country at the same time. Statesmen and political thinkers have on occasion noted the word's ambiguity, themselves deliberately using it in different contexts to convey a variety of meanings.[9]

This specialist in the history of the Russian Empire and in the comparative history of empires gives us a sketch of the rich and ambiguous history of the concept of empire and, against a global backdrop, describes the rise and fall of various major empires. The concept of empire was still linked with such concepts as prosperity and strength at the beginning of the twentieth century; its devaluation took place only during a distinct period in which Nazi Germany appropriated the concept of empire and when, during the Cold War, Western nations regularly used the term to castigate the Soviet Union. Why, however, did Western societies' repudiation of the Nazis and the Soviet Union rely on the condemnation of the concept of "empire"? In my opinion, this popular usage is based on a deeper intellectual background: in the categories of traditional political economy in the nineteenth century and in twentieth century social sciences, a connection had already been firmly established between empires' expansionism and despotism.[10] In this intellectual tradition, the devaluation of the concept of empire was the result of the nation-state system's establishment of its own hegemonic position, in which two oppositional relations are of utmost importance: first, an empire is a political system with vast territory, multiple ethnicities, and unlimited sovereignty, whereas the nation-state is a political system that functions in cases where there is a relatively small amount of territory, a homogenous ethnic group, and limited sovereignty. Second, in order to maintain control of vast territory and complex ethnic relations, empires tended toward despotic rule, whereas the nation-state, with its homogenous membership, tended more toward democratic or republican rule.

The intellectual sources of the empire/nation-state binary can be traced back to political-economic theory laid out in nineteenth-century European humanities. According to Habermas's account of the formation of the German nation-state:

> The worldview of the humanities . . . saw the political unification of Germany as the long-overdue realization of a national unity that had already developed on the level of culture. All that was missing from the body politic, itself defined through culture and language, was the appropriate political clothing. The linguistic community had to coincide with the legal community within one nation-state. Each nation, it seemed, possessed a claim to political independence as its birthright.[11]

The community established by culture and language, in essence, refers to the category of the nation or "people" so carefully defined in nineteenth-century "humanities" or "moral sciences"—the fields of philosophy, linguistics, and other types of political economy that were distinguished from the natural sciences during that period. For this category of the nation, the formation of the "appropriate political clothing"—the nation-state or legal community—formed a type of category of sovereignty for maintaining independence. Habermas's historical description gives us a classic version of how the nation-state describes itself, in which we can find a type of metanarrative that has yet to appear: the political independence of a nation or people points to an exclusive sovereign power to self-determination; this is a direct expression of monarchical states' rejection of the domination of the Holy Roman Empire. The combination of the nation and sovereignty created the conditions under which members of the nation could obtain equal rights as citizens because new trends in the nineteenth century defined a people or nation as an entity with an existence based on "natural characteristics" such as language, race, religion, faith, culture, and history; and yet the natural existence of the nation also possessed the power to establish a state and government with its own sovereignty. Under these conditions, the universal empire, with its vast territories and multiple nationalities, became a symbol of despotic political power that violated the laws of nature. For these reasons, the powers of a nation or people that were established by the humanities could only be established as such when placed in the opposition between empire and nation.

In nineteenth-century European thought, the previously described empire/nation-state binary serves not only as an account of political structures, but also as a generalization of the differences between the social-political systems of Europe and Asia, treating "empire" as an Asian political structure different from the political structure of European nations. Thus the empire/nation-state binary was intertwined with the Asia/Europe (or East/West) binary, providing a dual basis, in terms of both institutions and geography, for the establishment of Eurocentric nineteenth-century "world history." It is very clear that this theoretical understanding of Asian empires was produced through the self-recognition and authorization of Western European countries' political structures and their rationality. As Perry Anderson has shown, the so-called Asian state structure referred to in eighteenth- and nineteenth-century European thought—the despotic empire—emerged from European thinkers' observations of the power and influence of Turkey. As the first theorist to place the Ottoman state in opposition to European monarchies, Niccolo Machiavelli argued in *The Prince* that the monarchical bureaucracy of the Turkish state was a system utterly different from those of European states. After Machiavelli, Jean Bodin offered a now classic interpretation of European concepts of sovereignty based on an opposition between European "royal sovereignty" and Ottoman "lordly power." These two figures laid the foundation for a long-running tradition in which the state structures of European states were opposed to those of Asian states, thereby producing the concept of "Oriental despotism."[12] During the Enlightenment, however, Leibniz, Voltaire, and many other European thinkers showed virtually no trace of influence from this concept, but rather voiced the highest admiration for China and the Orient. Through missionary accounts, commercial activities, and interactions between the various courts, a number of figures from the Enlightenment drew inspiration from a variety of areas concerning China, including rational modes of living in Chinese society, management and planning of cities, mathematics and philosophy, and material culture. Their understanding of China, India, and other civilizations transformed into an important internal element of their "Enlightenment." The true influence of the previously described empire/nation-state binary was felt mostly during the latter portion of the eighteenth century and throughout the entire nineteenth century. The three major movements from this era were all made possible by the universalization of the empire/nation-state binary developed by Machiavelli and Bodin. First, the French Revolution and European and American national movements established a new model for political communities, providing political legitimacy for this binary. Second, colonialism created the historical preconditions for this binary to move from European history to a fundamental concept in a universal world history. Third, the nineteenth-century humanities and their intellectual development provided this binary with a framework of "objective knowledge" or "scientific knowledge."

Nineteenth-century European authors, inspired by developments in the natural sciences, attempted to apply the spirit and methods of science to their investigation of human societies. The binaries of empire/nation or empire/state were established in fields of knowledge such as philosophy, law, political theory, linguistics, anthropology, religion, and other fields gathered under the category of "political economy." Within the framework of European knowledge from this era, the concept of empire and its operations have the following characteristics: first, empire is a political-economic category that stands in opposition to the nation-state. Second, this oppositional relationship between empire and the nation-state was organized through a temporal relation, or, put another way, by a process of evolution in historical time that was organized in a way that takes political structures and economic models as its basic units. Third, this binary relationship of nation-state/empire can unfold into a temporal and spatial relationship between the West and non-West, i.e., the relationships between nation-states (the West) and empires (the non-West) can be interpreted using temporal categories such as "the present" and "the past" and "advanced" and "backward." The original comparison between Western European feudal states and the Ottoman Empire was transformed into a comparative relationship between European nation-states and Asian empires (Chinese, Islamic, Russian, Mughal, etc.): by demonstrating the historical linkages and discontinuities between Western European states and Asian empires, all characteristics of Europe—its states, laws, economies, languages, religions, philosophies, and geographical environments—gained opportunities for self-justification. These efforts toward European self-justification were predicated on an exceptionalist, universalist historiography and theory. As a result, it is today very difficult for us to understand that the despotic empires seen as unique to Asian countries are in fact derived from Europe's own understanding of the Ottoman Empire and Ottoman culture.[13] Against this backdrop, the nation-state becomes an essential characteristic of Europe and a cornerstone of "world history," while historical linkages are forged between the concept of empire and the geographical category of "Asia"—especially in terms of Islam, China, and the Mughals.

Within the antithetical relationship between Asia and Europe established by European writers such as Montesquieu, Adam Smith, G. W. F. Hegel, and Marx, the images of Asia and Europe are built up according to a teleological framework that opposes them to one another both in terms of political forms and economic forms: empire and nation-state, and agrarian economies and industrial or trade-based economies.[14] Within this dualistic framework, the concept of "Asia" possesses the following characteristics: it is ruled by multiethnic empires, which stand in contrast to the early modern European states or monarchies; it is dominated by political despotism, which stands in contrast to early modern European legal and political systems; and it is dependent on nomadic or agrarian modes of production, which are completely different from urban life and trade in Europe. It is only when we begin from this perspective that we can understand the narratives and rhetorical strategies concerning China that were employed by European thinkers of this era. Montesquieu, for example, rejected out of hand some of the relatively positive accounts about Chinese politics, law, customs, and culture that came from missionaries and from discussions in the European Enlightenment (the same accounts that had provided inspiration for positive discussions of China by Voltaire and Leibniz). Instead, Montesquieu used the concepts of "despotism" and "empire" to characterize the entire political culture of China.[15] According to his classic account, the main characteristic of an empire is that the paramount ruler uses military force to monopolize the power to distribute property, thereby wiping out any aristocratic systems that might balance out autocratic rule and suppressing the emergence of separate nation-states. This narrative not only lacks any discussion of individual characteristics of such "Asian empires" as the Ottoman Empire, Mughal Empire, Russian Empire, or Qing dynasty, but also admits no possibility for societies to be produced by interaction or by hybrid relationships. As imagined by Montesquieu, none of the wars, conquests, or many interactions between societies that took place in Chinese history could change the fact that the society was an empire. In his words: "Conquest does not make China lose its laws. As manners, mores, laws, and religion are but the same thing there."[16] This view was very similar to opinions about China held by the early missionaries such as Jean Baptiste Du Halde (1674–1743), who argued that China's politics, laws, language, clothing, morality, and customs had maintained their unity over the previous four millennia without undergoing any essential changes. According to this "culturalist" outlook, which omitted historical changes or historical interactions, Asia has no history and lacks the historical conditions and forces needed to produce modernity—the core of modernity is "the state" and its laws, as well as urban and trade-oriented ways of life.

In a series of foundational narratives from the eighteenth and nineteenth centuries, the concept of "Asia" is closely linked with despotic imperial systems that covered broad swaths of territory and multiple ethnic groups. These two categories are produced precisely in antithesis to the Greek republic and the European form of the monarchical state—amid the course of nineteenth-century movements for democracy, the Republican system and the feudal monarchical state were both seen as ancestors to the European nation-state, and this type of European nation-state was differentiated from any other unique political form found in other geographical regions. In this discourse of self-legitimation, the imperial system (Ottoman, Chinese, Mughal, Russian, and other large, multinational empires), serving as the political form of Oriental despotism, was unable to produce the political structures needed to enable capitalist development[17] or the economic rationalism that, according to Weber, originated in Protestant ethics. Early modern capitalism, then, was the product of Western Europe's unique social system. Inevitable and natural linkages, then, could be found between capitalist development and the nation-state system that took the feudal state as its historical precursor. Intentionally or unintentionally, this discourse overlooks the fact that, to this day, all political systems are the result of interactions taking place across history, and that the Roman Empire, the Islamic empires, the Chinese empire, and other imperial forms were precisely the most important medium for "globalization before globalization." Even if they offer deep insights, then, discourses that treat modernity as the result of a single culture or set of institutional conditions are highly reductive.

Because the expansion of the European nation-state and capitalist market system have been seen as a higher stage and goal of world history, Asia (and the previously described characteristics that have been attributed to it) has been seen as a lower stage of world history. In this context, Asia is not only a geographical category but also a civilizational form. It represents a political form antithetical to the European nation-state, a social form antithetical to European capitalism, and a kind of transitional form that involves passage from the state of lacking history toward the state of being in history. If we say the empire/nation-state binary places particular emphasis on accounts of political structures and models of identity, and that the Asia/Europe binary places particular emphasis on accounts of geographical relations, then the framework of civilizational differences organizes the political structures, models of identity, and previously described geographical relationships into a temporal logic of "traditional" versus "modern." On the one hand, in the Western context of transition from feudal state to nation-state, extremely close links exist between the concept of despotism and the concept of a far-reaching empire, and thus "the nation-state," as a category antithetical to empire, achieves a superior status both in value and in history. On the other hand, as European capitalism gradually spread over the entire globe, this binary between empire and nation-state also became an implied structure through which Europe or the West established its own identity and its own "world history." European intellectuals, Asian revolutionaries and reformers, and historians all used this narrative of Asian empires and European nation-states as a basic framework to describe world history and Asian societies; to establish blueprints for revolution and reform; and to sketch out Asia's past and future. Across much of the nineteenth and twentieth centuries, narratives of Asian empires were implied in narratives of universal European modernity, providing relatively similar narrative frameworks for both colonialists and revolutionaries, even as they laid out blueprints for the future that were often sharply opposed to one another. The three central themes and key concepts of this framework were empire, the nation-state, and capitalism (market economies). From the nineteenth century to the present, virtually all discourses on Asia are linked in one way or another with these three central themes and key concepts. The image of Asian agrarian empires, then, was also produced through the process by which Europeans of the eighteenth and nineteenth centuries formed a new European identity.

In nineteenth-century European discourses of history, philosophy, law, the state, and religion, the empire/nation-state binary not only formed into a structural antithetical relationship, but also was drawn into a teleological view of time. European "world history," then, could be summarized as a kind of temporal narrative structured around the evolution of political forms. In the German metaphysical tradition, this universal history focused on political forms was included in the intellectual framework provided by nineteenth-century German "human sciences" or "moral sciences" (*Geisteswissenschaften*). For example, G. W. F. Hegel, inspired by discoveries about the links between European languages and Sanskrit that had been made by European linguists, connected these historical linkages between languages with two other major developments in nineteenth-century European knowledge—theories of race and historical geography. He then argued that Asian empires should be seen as the earliest historical starting point for the emergence of European states:

> It is a great discovery in history—as of a new world—which has been made within rather more than the last twenty years, respecting the Sanskrit and the connection of the European languages with it. In particular, the connection of the German and Indian peoples has been demonstrated, with as much certainty as such subjects allow of. Even at the present time we know of peoples that scarcely form a society, much less a State, but that have been long known as existing. . . . In the connection just referred to, between the languages of nations so widely separated, we have a result before us, which proves the diffusion of those nations from Asia as a center, and the so dissimilar development of what had been originally related, as an incontestable fact.[18]

According to this argument, Asia could serve as the "starting point" under two conditions. First, Asia and Europe are organic parts linked together in the same unified historical process; otherwise, there would be no question of a starting point or end point. Second, Asia and Europe are positioned at utterly different stages of this process of historical development, and that which forms the basis for making this judgment about stages is, by and large, "the state." The reason that Asia is positioned at the "starting point" or in a period that lacks history is that it is not a state and has not yet formed into a subject of history. In this sense, when the Asian region transforms into "states," then Asia is no longer Asia—the category of "Asia" in itself is no more than a symbolic expression of the process by which "Absolute Spirit" returns to its originary state. To demonstrate the history of the development of Absolute Spirit, Hegel argued that a "geographical basis of history" was required, a space in which "Spirit" could emerge. The form of geography, then, structured "time" as "space":

> In the History of the World, the Idea of Spirit appears in its actual
> embodiment as a series of external forms, each one of which de-
> clares itself as an actually existing people. This existence falls
> under the category of Time as well as Space, in the way of natural
> existence.[19]

According to this "philosophical history," which organized "space" as
"time" or treated "time" as "space," the development of Absolute Spirit
passed through four major historical stages, including the "Oriental world,"
which included China, India, and Persia; the "Greek world"; the "Roman
world"; and the "German world," which represented the modern world.
The German world is the repetition of all previous worlds, the return of
Absolute Spirit to its original state. Asia's surface characteristic is that it is
the Eastern part of the globe, it is a place of origin, and its deep structure
is the despotic empire. It is only in this implicit contrast between empire
and state that Hegel is able to present Europe, which had been produced in Asia, as the center and terminus of the old world, or the "Absolute West":

> The History of the World travels from East to West, for Europe is
> absolutely the end of History, Asia the beginning. . . . History has
> a determinate East, viz. Asia. . . . The East knew and to the pres-
> ent day knows only that *One* is free; the Greek and Roman world,
> that *some* are free; the German world knows that *All* are free. The
> first political form therefore which we observe in History is *Des-
> potism*, the second *Democracy* and *Aristocracy*, and the third
> *Monarchy.*[20]

Why was Hegel able to convert "time" into "space" so naturally,
and then offer an interpretation of the development of Spirit through
the categories of "world history" and state political systems? From the
internal logic and intellectual premises of Hegel's theory, this conversion can only take place under two conditions. First, a major source of
Hegel's philosophy of history is a psychological theory that developed
out of an individualist and anthropocentric tradition. The goal of this
psychological theory is to resolve philosophical difficulties produced by

individualist discourse by using a construct of analogical relationships between world history and history of individual spirit. As a universal unit of analysis, the individual imagines the world and its unlimited richness as the history of the universal subject, whereas political forms— that is, state forms based on despotic forms of government, democratic forms of government, and aristocratic forms of government—serve as markers of stages on a timeline of the process of the self-emergence of this universal subject. It is precisely from within this anthropocentric and political-formalist tradition that Hegel is able to understand different geographical regions and historical forms as part a process of the development of Spirit, and thereby overcome questions surrounding social disintegration produced by the expansion of markets, the division of labor, and individualism.[21] For Hegel, the individual and state, which are commonly placed in antithetical positions in European thought, both become subordinate to a larger process of historical progress. Hegel borrowed from Adam Smith's category of "civil society" (as well as property rights and contractual relationships directly related to markets), but the core of his political philosophy was the role of the state, the field of politics, and national identity. Nineteenth-century Germans lived in a weak and disintegrating state and lacked a political medium that could provide a framework for unifying German culture. It was under these circumstances that Hegel placed the system of the state and its laws at the highest level of historical progress, responding to the political and social realities of a divided Germany that had been in effect since the sixteenth century (and that were especially prominent in the eighteenth century) with a concept of a type of democracy based on a unitary state. Under this model, civil society and the political culture of the state would unify multiple identities drawn apart by affinities to clan, region, and religion. Hegel's philosophy's revival of "wholeness" was a revival of the wholeness of the state, whose function was to provide a political structure for civil society and to overcome the divisions created between people by the market and its divisions of labor. In Hegel's view, when separated from the state and its legal institutions, atomized individuals in bourgeois society were unable to coalesce into a civil society:

> The selfish end in its actualization, conditioned in this way by universality, establishes a system of all-around interdependence, so that the subsistence and welfare of the individual and his rightful existence are interwoven with, and grounded on, the subsistence, welfare, and rights of all, and have actuality and security only in this context.—One may regard this system in the first instance as the *external state,* the *state of necessity,* and *of the understanding.*[22]

Second, if we compare the narratives of Oriental, Greek, Roman, and Germanic stages of history in Hegel's philosophy of history with the four stages of history proposed in Adam Smith's economic history—from nomadic, to pastoral, to agrarian, and then to commercial—then we quickly discover that Hegel's account of historical stages based on political forms has clear internal linkages with Smith's account of historical stages based on modes of production. According to Smith, the development from agrarian society to commercial society took place during Europe's transition from feudal society to a modern market society. In this account, then, Smith used a form of historical narrative to create internal linkages between the modern, commercial era and European society. On the one hand, Smith was a historian: his accounts of the economy were a kind of historical account. On the other hand, however, his model for the operations of the market was an abstract process: the discovery of the Americas, colonialism, and rising class divisions were all described in an economic account of endless market expansion, division of labor, industrial progress, and growth of taxation and wealth. Within this formalist narrative, a discourse on the cyclical operations of global markets was established. Thus in Smith's view the model of the market is the result of historical development and is also an inherent historical principle; the specific spatial relationships of colonialism and social division are transformed into a temporal process of production, circulation, and consumption. The convertibility of time and space is premised on the historical linkages between the production processes of capitalism and the regional relationships of colonialism: on the one hand, in Smith's account of the processes of the movement of capital, the temporal relations between production, circulation, and consumption can only be completed through such spatial movements as colonialism abroad, class division, and market expansion. On the other hand, these spatial relationships that are structured by the division of labor are not external to the relationships of the continuous movement of capital, and thus the geography of spatial relations can be transformed into the temporal relations found in market activities. It is worth noting that it is precisely in Smith's account of the repetition of production and exchange that Hegel discovers that the process of cyclical movement itself produces both class divisions and imperialism: the endless expansion of production and consumption processes inevitably leads to population growth, limitations on the division of labor, and divisions between classes, forcing civil society to expand beyond its own borders, seek out new markets, and implement colonial policies:

> By exposing the pursuit of gain to danger, industry simultaneously rises above it; and for the ties of the soil and the limited circles of civil life with its pleasures and desires, it substitutes the element of fluidity, danger, and destruction. Through this supreme medium of communication, it also creates trading links with distant countries, a legal relationship which gives rise to contracts; and at the same time, such trade is the greatest educational asset and the source from which commerce derives its world-historical significance.[23]

Thus Hegel interprets the links between civil society, economic activity, consumerism, and the expansion of imperialism as "the world-historical significance" of commerce, thereby providing the conditions under which he can gather civil society, the market economy, legal philosophy, and science of the state into his framework of the development of "world history" or "Absolute Spirit."[24]

According to Hegel's framework of "world history," a civil society made up of free individuals and the legal system of civil society provide the internal structure for the formation of political community (the state). This political community is not a purely man-made construct, but rather the product of a comprehensive process of evolution, and thus forms the ultimate goal of "world history."[25] Hegel's concept of the Orient is a philosophical response to discourses on the Orient in European thought; at its core, it is a comparison of European state structures and Asian state structures. Because Hegel's discussion of civil society, markets, and trade is based on Scottish political economy, his notion of a despotic Asia echoes discussions of specific economic systems. In *The Wealth of Nations,* Smith mentions the connections between hydrology projects and the agrarian character of China and other Asian countries, distinguishing them from characteristics of European urban industries, especially manufacturing and foreign trade. His designation of the historical stages of nomadic, pastoral, agrarian, and commercial also serves to categorize the conditions of different geographical regions and peoples. For example, when he discusses "nations of hunters" in "the lowest and rudest state of society," Smith refers to the "native tribes of North America"; his accounts of people in "a more advanced state of society" points to "Tartars and Arabs"; when he discusses peoples in a "yet more advanced state of society," he again refers to the ancient Greeks and Romans (earlier sections also refer to agriculture in China). Commercial societies for Smith are the "civilized states" of Europe.[26] Smith sees the transition from agrarian society to commercial society as European feudal societies' transition to a modern market society, and thus the modern, commercial era bears implicit historical links to European society. It is precisely for this reason that what is ultimately produced by Smith's analysis of the historical relationships between Europe and other regions is a narrative of economic operations. Smith argues, for example, that Europe gains the following benefits from the discovery and colonization of the Americas:

> First, in the increase of its enjoyments; and secondly, in the augmentation of its industry. . . . The discovery and colonization of America, it will readily be allowed, have contributed to augment the industry, first, of all the countries which trade to it directly; such as Spain, Portugal, France, and England; and, secondly, all of those which, without trading to it directly, send, through the medium of other countries, goods to it of their own produce; such as Austrian Flanders, and some provinces of Germany, which, through the medium of the countries before mentioned, send to it a considerable quantity of linen and other goods. All such countries have evidently gained a more extensive market for their surplus produce, and must consequently have been encouraged to increase its quantity.[27]

Smith linked the discovery of the Americas and its effect on Europe very closely with the unlimited expansion of markets, division of labor, industrial progress, and growth in taxes and wealth, thereby including the expansion of colonialism and the global relations between geographical regions in a discourse concerning the cyclical activities of world markets.

From Hegel's perspective, all of these questions can be seen in terms of the politics of the state: the reason that nomadic peoples can be seen as the "lowest and rudest" peoples is because the scale of hunter-gatherer groups is relatively small, and they have no way to produce the kind of political division of labor that structures the state. In Ernest Gellner's words, "For them, the question of the state, of the stable, specialized order-enforcing institution, does not really arise."[28] For this reason, then, Hegel's account of "world history" categorically excludes all of North America (which is characterized by hunter-gatherer ways of living), and places the Orient—with its imperial political system and agrarian mode of production—at the beginning point of history. If Smith divided history into different forms of economies or production, then Hegel determined different historical forms according to geography, civilization, and state structure. Both, however, linked forms of production or political forms with specific spaces (such as Asia, America, Africa, Europe), organizing them into a set of temporal relationships determined by stages of history. As Angus Walker wrote:

> Although the Scottish writers subscribed to Smith's view that it was the division of labor which impelled society toward greater wealth and diversity of activity, economic, social, and intellectual, they were all . . . well aware that the division of labor . . . could have adverse social effects. This negative aspect of progress is never the major theme of their work. . . . What, in Scottish hands, was a reasonably optimistic account of progress was used by German writers as an explanation of their own fragmentation. The division of labor was seen as the reason for the stratification of society, for the specialization of man's activities which deprived him of that full exercise of all his powers, mental and physical, for which nature had destined him. It accounted for the weakening of social and personal bonds and for a decline in the coherence of society.[29]

Regardless of whatever position they start from, when faced with the question of whether or not Asia has its own history, these authors all respond in the negative, because history must have a subject, and in nineteenth-century European political discourse, that subject is the nation-state. In this sense, this response to the question was not produced by specific historical accounts of Asia or China, but rather was produced by the construct of "world history," or produced by the construct in which Europe lies at the "end" of "world history." As the starting point of history, Asia represents a form in which agrarian modes of production are organized under an imperial political structure, whereas as the "end" of history, Europe represents the universal rule in which capitalism is placed under the political structure of the nation-state. Through what logic, then, did this principle of history come to be "naturalized"?

Marx's account of the transformation of the economic structure of society used four historical stages—Asiatic, primitive, feudal, and bourgeois—thereby revealing that his concept of a unique Asiatic mode of production was produced through a synthesis of Smith's and Hegel's views of history. According to Perry Anderson, Marx's idea of the "Asiatic mode of production" was largely based on a series of accounts coming out of European thought since the fifteenth century that focused on the uniqueness of Asia: the system of state ownership of land (James Harrington, Bernier, Montesquieu), the lack of legal restrictions (Bodin, Montesquieu, Bernier), the usurpation of law by religion (Montesquieu), the lack of a hereditary aristocracy (Machiavelli, Bacon, Montesquieu), social equality and leveling that bordered on slavery (Montesquieu, Hegel), isolated villages (Hegel), the suppression of industry by overreliance on agriculture (John Stuart Mill, Bernier), irrigation and hydraulic works by the state (Hegel, Mill), a hot and arid climate (Montesquieu, Mill), and historical stasis (Montesquieu, Hegel, Mill).[30] All of these writers took these various characteristics to be expressions of Oriental despotism. This line of thinking, in turn, could be traced back to conclusions made about Asia in Greek thought:

> The definite emergence of the notion of "despotism," moreover, co-
> incided with its extrojection onto the "Orient" from the start. For

the central canonical passage in classical Antiquity where the original Greek word itself (an unusual term) can be found was a famous statement by Aristotle: "Barbarians are more servile by nature than Greeks, and Asians are more servile than Europeans; hence they endure despotic rule without protest. Such monarchies are like tyrannies, but they are secure because they are hereditary and legal."[31]

The idea of the "servile" nature of Asians was derived from historical observations about the stability of the structure of ancient societies, even though the very deep, internal, revolutionary changes that occurred time and again in the structure of Asian societies—including the structure of Chinese society—are completely absent from the field of vision in these versions of history. Anderson did not mention whether or not Marx drew from Adam Smith's account of modes of production, and also did not consider how Marx's historical-materialist position incorporated Hegel's logic of history, which was based on a superstructure, into his own framework of the transformation of modes of production, and thereby overturned the relationship between superstructure and base found in Hegel's thought. Marx's incorporation of aspects of Smith and Hegel, as well as his "overturning" of Hegel, still did not overturn the fundamental logic within European political thought that provided a route for placing political forms and modes of production onto a temporal sequence.

The various theories of national self-determination that developed in the early twentieth century (Leninism and Wilsonianism) were all subordinated to this temporal logic that was based on the political form of the state. In Lenin's framework for understanding capitalism and world revolution, efforts made by backward regions (Asian agrarian empires) to change their own social structure and to pursue capitalist development also became key internal elements in a "world revolution" against the capitalist system. This new interpretation of "world history," however, was still predicated on the empire/nation-state and agrarian/industrial-commercial binaries because Lenin's hope for revolution in Asia and his critique of European capitalism were all completely based on the central idea that the model of national self-determination created the conditions for capitalist development. Not long after the overthrow of the Qing dynasty in 1911 and the establishment of the provisional Chinese government in 1912, Lenin published works such as "Democracy and Narodnism in China" (1912), "The Awakening of Asia" (1913), and "Backward Europe and Advanced Asia" (1913). He declared that "China [was] a land of seething political activity, the scene of a virile social movement and of a democratic upsurge,"[32] and excoriated Europe, "with its highly developed machine industry, its rich multiform culture, and its constitutions," which, under the leadership of the bourgeoisie, "support[ed] . . . everything backward, moribund, and medieval."[33] This assessment was a prototype of a theory that Lenin would later develop on imperialism and proletarian revolution. In his view, when capitalism entered the imperialist phase, the social struggles undertaken by oppressed peoples from around the world would coalesce into a global proletarian revolution. This move to discuss European revolutions and Asian revolutions in the same frame can be traced to an 1853 article written by Marx for the *New York Daily Tribune*, "Revolution in China and Europe." The conclusions drawn by Lenin, quite opposite to those of Fukuzawa Yukichi's call to "shed Asia," were based on the premise (also found in Fukuzawa's argument) that Asia's early modernity was the product of Europe's early modernity; regardless of Asia's status or fate, the significance of this early modernity could only be expressed through its relationship with early modern Europe. For example, Lenin argued that Russia should be seen as an Asian state, but based his argument not on geography, but rather on the degree of capitalist development and on Russia's historical development. In "Democracy and Narodnism in China," he wrote: "In very many and very essential respects Russia is undoubtedly an Asiatic country, and, moreover, one of the wildest, most medieval, and shamefully backward of Asiatic countries."[34] Even if Lenin sympathized deeply with the Chinese revolution, when the question turns from Asian revolutions to the question of revolution in Russian society, his position is nonetheless that of the "Westernizers," not the "Slavophiles."[35] What exactly, then, makes up the characteristics of this "Asian state"? A despotic empire, agriculture, and peasant serfdom. Nineteenth- and twentieth-century Russian intellectuals saw the Russian spirit as a site of collision and struggle between the forces of East and West and between Asia and Europe. In the quotations just given, Asia is yoked together with such concepts as barbarism, the medieval, and backwardness, yet it is precisely because of these associations that the Russian Revolution has such a deeply Asian character—because the revolution is directed against "wild, medieval, and shamefully backward" social relations, which are also characteristics of "Asian states"— and possesses global significance.

The October Revolution of 1917 took place against the immediate background of World War I and also had a deep influence on subsequent Chinese revolutionary activities. Two important facts, however, are often overlooked. First, the October Revolution happened after the 1911 Chinese revolution that overthrew the Qing dynasty, and the socialist state building that began with the October Revolution can be seen to a very large degree as a response to Asian revolutions (including the 1911 Chinese revolution). Lenin's theory of national self-determination and his interpretation of revolutions in backward states during the era of imperialism all took shape after the 1911 Chinese revolution and have theoretical linkages to his analysis of the Chinese revolution. The logic of using the state form to respond to the challenges posed by European capitalism did not in itself have any relation to Marx or nineteenth-century socialist theory, but rather was established on the basis of the empire/ nation-state binary. According to the historical framework of this binary, the state is the most important condition for capitalist development and for the formation of civil society. Socialists merely injected Hegel's dialectical logic into this binary: it is only with the state form, they argued, that it is possible to provide the impetus to move beyond the state form. In other words, only the conditions of production and organizational methods of capitalism can provide those conditions of production and organizational methods that exceed capitalism. The combination of socialism and the state was both an effort to overturn the "world history" structured by the combination of state forms and modes of production in nineteenth-century European thought and an expression of the revolutionary nature of the logic internal to this world history. Second, the Russian Revolution shocked Europe deeply; the revolution can be seen as an event that severed Russia and Europe from one another. Throughout the period from the October Revolution through World War II and the Cold

War, Russia (the Soviet Union), when viewed from a Western European perspective that was based on the opposition between East and West, was seen as returning to Asia's embrace; the short-term wartime alliances that formed during World War II could not alter this perception. There was no fundamental difference between Lenin's assessment of revolution and accounts of Asia already provided by Smith and Hegel: all three men understood the history of capitalism as a historical process in which the ancient Orient evolved toward the ways of modern Europe—an inevitable development characterized by the transformation of modes of production from nomadic and agrarian toward the commercial and the industrial. For Lenin, however, this framework of world history began to have a dual significance. On the one hand, global capitalism and the social movements it touched off in Russia in 1905 were a fundamental force in the awakening of Asia[36]—a land that for so long had been completely static and without history. On the other hand, the Chinese revolution represented the most advanced phenomenon in world history, which socialists could use to show a clear path that would lead away from the imperialist world system. The long-running debates that broke out between the "Slavophile" and "Westernizing" schools of Russian intellectuals and revolutionaries can, from a certain perspective, show the dual historical significance that lies behind the discourse on Asia.[37]

This special status of Asia and its political-economic forms in the rhetoric of world history also played a decisive role in how socialists understood the mission and direction of modern Asian revolutions. The October Revolution created a scenario in which the systems of socialism and capitalism stood opposed to one another, but Lenin's theory nonetheless extended the historical affirmation of capitalism made by Smith, Hegel, and Marx. The central question on which Lenin focused was how to create a political structure in Russia and in Asia that would be capable of providing the conditions for capitalist development. In the end, the question of national self-determination was really a question of how to develop capitalism. In his assessment of proposals for democracy beyond capitalism and socialism put forward by Chinese revolutionaries, Lenin criticized these proposals for their vacuousness and argued that they were in fact a form of Narodnism. In his opinion, "The chief representative or the main social support of this Asiatic bourgeoisie, which is still capable of performing historically progressive deeds, is the peasant,"[38] and therefore the peasantry first must complete the revolutionary mission of the European bourgeoisie before discussions about the problems of socialism could begin. On the one hand, Lenin skillfully employed historical dialectics, condemning Sun Yat-sen's land reform program as "counterrevolutionary," because it diverted from or exceeded the stages of history. On the other hand, he also pointed out that because of the "Asian" nature of Chinese society, this "counterrevolutionary program" in fact achieved the mission of capitalism: "By the irony of history, Narodnism, in the name of the 'struggle against capitalism' in agriculture, advocates an agrarian program which, if fully realized, would mean the *most* rapid development of capitalism in agriculture."[39] It is very clear that an understanding of Asia determined, in part, their understanding of the tasks and direction of revolution. What, then, were the preconditions for Lenin's views on Asia? It was the unique role assigned to Asia in Hegel's and Smith's views on world history (i.e., an agrarian Asia that is medieval, barbaric, and has no history), combined with the logic of capitalism and revolution. This "Hegel + Revolution" view of Asia contained a model of historical development that proceeded from the ancient (feudalism) to the medieval (capitalism) and to the modern (proletarian revolution or socialism). This view also provided a framework of temporality and stages of progression with which those in the capitalist era could understand the history of other geographical regions.

These two views of Asia work from different directions to provide ways to understand historical connections between capitalism and the concept of Asia. Within these historical connections we can see clearly the oppositions between empire and nation-state and agriculture and industry. The theory of national self-determination developed by Lenin in 1914 understood colonialism and social revolutions as two utterly opposed transnational and international forces in the modern world. At the same time, however, his theory also saw these two forces as the basis of national self-determination or the basis for the creation of the political form that enabled the development of capitalism—i.e., the nation-state. Why did those revolutions that flew the flag of internationalism and socialism also set their course toward the historical form of the nation-state? According to Lenin,

> The national state is the rule and the "norm" of capitalism; the multinational state represents backwardness, or is an exception. . . . This does not mean, of course, that such a state, which is based on bourgeois relations, can eliminate the exploitation and oppression of nations. It only means that Marxists cannot lose sight of the powerful *economic* factors that give rise to the urge to create national states. It means that "self-determination of nations" in the Marxists' Program *cannot,* from a historico-economic point of view, have any other meaning than political self-determination, state independence, and the formation of a national state.[40]

Thus we see an opposition between the "nation-state" and the "multinational state" (or "empire"), with the former as the "norm" of capitalism and the latter as the pole opposed to the nation-state. National self-determination is "political self-determination"; this idea implies that national self-determination is not simply a return to identity politics, but is in a political sense the exercise of self-determination, which forms the political conditions for the development of capitalist economics—i.e., the political structure of the political nation or nation-state. Therefore, when Lenin speaks of "the awakening of Asia," his concerns lie not in problems of socialism, but in the question of how to create the political conditions for the development of capitalism from within the relationship between agriculture and empire, or, in other words, the problem of how to create (industrial and market-oriented) capitalism's political structure and model for the division of labor—the nation-state. Lenin welcomed the fact that "capitalism, having awakened Asia, has called forth national movements everywhere in that continent, too; that the tendency of these movements is towards the creation of national states in Asia; that it is such states that ensure the best conditions for the development of capitalism."[41] He very clearly points out the internal connections between nationalism and capitalism: it is neither revolution nor the unique cultures of Asia that demands national movements, but the development of capitalism. Once we have understood the relationship between Lenin's theories of revolution and national self-determination on the one hand and nineteenth-century European political economy on the other—especially the deeply rooted binary between empire and nation-state—it is then possible to understand structural similarities in the problems that occur in interpretations of Chinese modernity made both by Chinese Marxists (who found a theoretical basis for many of their arguments in Leninism) and by the Fairbank school. If we synthesize their analyses of China's national and social crises, then we can see three broad similarities between their arguments. First, China's crisis is the crisis of an empire with vast territory, multiple ethnicities, and major differences in regional cultures. Second, governing an empire depends upon a strong and unified central state; this is, in fact, the source of China's crisis. Third, a unified central state is predicated on a specific political culture, and this political culture is founded upon Confucian culture (and the written Chinese language). Thus we can infer the following: the crisis is a crisis of a unified empire, and unified empires always tend toward using centralized power to govern the state. Methods that lead to the disintegration of despotism, then, will also lead to the disintegration of this empire and its political culture. National self-determination, then, is the main way to resolve the problem of despotism.[42]

The empire/nation-state binary in nineteenth- and twentieth-century European thought was produced in a universalist system of knowledge; it spread out across many fields, including political science, economics, law, cultural anthropology, linguistics, archaeology, history, and racial theory. Across a number of national movements and state-building projects, this process of structuring knowledge played an extremely important role: to imagine or structure Japan as a modern nation-state, Japanese society engaged in continuous and large-scale translation and introduction of Western politics, law, and science from the Meiji reforms onward. To transform the political structure of Czarist Russia and its relations with the world, Lenin repeatedly read Hegel and Marx in great detail as he designed his theory of national self-determination. To undertake reform within the Manchu Qing empire or to overturn the imperial system and establish a republic, all varieties of movements since the late Qing engaged in unprecedented translation, introduction, and interpretation of

Western politics, law, economics, and cultural theory. Nationalist knowledge and thinking induced the birth of state-centered and popular nationalist movements. This phenomenon tells us that the imagination,
planning, and design of the nation-state all have deep connections to a
type of universalist knowledge (or, more accurately, a type of particular-
ist universalism). Virtually all types of nationalist thought—whether they
appear in the form of popular social movements; official actions toward
political, legal, and economic reform; or expression of sentiment, literary
art, or religious faith—are predicated on this type of universalist worldview and system of knowledge. Within this universalist system of knowledge, knowledge of the state becomes the center of historical and political narratives. Therefore, aside from social conditions, the emergence of
national movements driven by the masses or popular sovereignty and
state-building movements based on political sovereignty all bear internal
connections to certain epistemological frameworks. In the following section I will begin to address this issue.

THREE

Heavenly Principle/Universal Principle and History

1. TIME AND PROPENSITY OF TIME

In *The Rise of Modern Chinese Thought,* questions about the relationships between empire and nation-state and between systems of enfeoffment *(fengjian)* and centralized administration *(junxian)* emerge from a
more fundamental line of thought in intellectual history: the establishment
of "Heavenly Principle" *(tianli)* and the changes in intellectual thought that
unfolded through transformations in the relationships between "principle"
(li) and "things" *(wu).*[1] The first half of *The Rise of Modern Chinese Thought*
discusses the significance of this issue in the context of Confucian thought,
and the second half continues with observations of the formation of the
scientific worldview and its internal contradictions. The problem of the relationship between "principle" and "things" addresses the themes of
change and stasis and continuity and discontinuity—that is, the problem
of "the order of things" and its natural unfolding. Within this framework,
all of the political and social problematics previously discussed can be
seen as the historical form of this order and its unfolding. The discussion
of the worldviews of Heavenly Principle and the axiomatic Universal
Principle is actually an inquiry into unique characteristics of, historical
changes in, and claims to legitimacy made for Chinese identity in different eras. Simply put, the Heavenly Principle, as a universal set of values
for a moral-political community, is the key concept for moral-ethical

praxis, cultural identity, and political legitimacy in China "before the West." The disintegration of a worldview based on Heavenly Principle meant that this moral-political community and its sense of identity that took shape over a long stretch of history fell into crisis. As the result of this disintegration, the emergence of the Universal Principle/scientific worldview indicates that previously extant forms of identity had already become difficult to maintain. Alongside the expansion of the capitalist-colonialist system, the nation-state model then becomes a dominant political form. In the midst of China's own transformation, the traditional historical-political identity of the hybrid state cannot but give way to a kind of newly emergent form of identity found in a national identity that takes shape within the framework of the worldview of Universal Principle. In cases ranging from early nationalist ideology's dependence on the worldview of Universal Principle to the implicit connections between Universal Principle and the Chinese Communist movement and its ideology, it becomes clear that the Heavenly Principle worldview and the model of identity that it embodied could no longer provide a legitimate basis for Chinese identity.

Just as the worldview of Heavenly Principle resisted and even defeated the dominant influences of Buddhism, Taoism, and local religions with its ability to structure common sense in daily life, cosmology, epistemology, and ritual practice, the modern scientific worldview (or worldview of Universal Principle) challenged the dominant position of the worldview of Heavenly Principle through the structuring of its cosmology, historiography, and methodology, as well as its appeal to common sense. In a large number of documents from the late Qing to the "May Fourth" era, we can sense the sharp opposition between the worldviews of Heavenly Principle and Universal Principle. First, Universal Principle reversed the view of history presented by Heavenly Principle, locating the realization of an ideal politics and morality not in the past but in the future. This reversal collapsed the sense of historical truncation or discontinuity embedded within the Confucian worldview, along with the will to produce connections and continuity with tradition that were produced by this sensibility, substituting this consciousness with another historical consciousness that emphasized the continuity of history and endless evolution—and the will to break from the past that is produced by this consciousness. Under the dominance of this historical consciousness, the primary emphasis is not a construction of traditional orthodoxy through individual moral-political practices, but the commitment to the project of the future; this commitment expresses a historical will to produce a new ethics. Second, the worldview of Universal Principle substituted concepts of the "propensity of the times" (shishi) and the "propensity of principle" (li shi) found in the worldview of Heavenly Principle with a linear concept of time that extends into the future.[2] Concepts of the "propensity of the times" and the "propensity of principle" are internal to the transformation of material things and do not weave the transformation of material things into a teleological timeline. Linear time, however, provides a teleological framework that brings the entirety of changes, transformations, and developments of the Lebenswelt into a teleological sequence. Third, the worldview of Universal Principle structured the category of "fact" in a teleological way to attack the metaphysical assumptions of the worldview of Heavenly Principle, attempting to use the logic of the fact or natural principles as a basis for structuring ethics and politics. With the establishment of this atomistic notion of facts, any resistance to the logic of facts or natural principles was forced to recognize the binary between facts and values. This ethical orientation stood directly in opposition to previous efforts to overcome the binaries of Cheng-Zhu neo-Confucian orthodoxy that had been undertaken by such thinkers as Lu Xiangshan (1139–1193), Gu Yanwu (1613–1682), and Zhang Xuecheng (1738–1801) in the fields of "learning of the heard-mind" (xinxue), studies of the classics, and studies of history.

However, in its critique of neo-Confucianism, the modern "worldview of scientific Universal Principle" also adopted the vision of the natural order found in neo-Confucianism. When comparing the moralism of Thomas Huxley (1825–1895) and the naturalism of Herbert Spencer (1820–1903), Yan Fu (1854–1921) explained the differences between the two by making direct reference to the "Theory of Heaven" (tian lun) as discussed by Liu Zongyuan (773–819) and Liu Yuxi (772–842), undertaking a "naturalist" critique of evolutionary ideas such as "natural selection" and "survival of the fittest" through an application of the model of the "Theory of Heaven."[3] Starting with modern theories of evolution, Yan Fu worked his way back to the theories of Heaven put forward by Liu Zongyuan and Liu Yuxi, linking his version of the concept of natural selection *(wujing tianze)* with Liu Yuxi's argument that "the myriad things are regarded as limitless . . . because each has the advantage in its own sphere and each functions by turn in its own sphere."[4] Yan Fu believed that these links revealed a basic historical fact: even from within the historical outlook found in evolutionary thought, the grounds on which the "Theory of Heaven" served as a basis of legitimacy for the existing order of reality had not changed.[5] At the same time, Yan Fu followed Zhu Xi's logic of "investigating things and extending knowledge" *(gewu zhi zhi)* to understand the significance of scientific methods and to attempt to unify scientific knowledge with moral and ethical practice. For these reasons, the decline of the Heavenly Principle worldview and the rise of the scientific worldview are not a simple relation of succession and supplanting; deep entanglements bind the two. For example, the category of "the transformations of heaven" *(tianyan)*, the term that Yan Fu used to translate "evolution," understands modern states, societies, markets, and many categories of rights and powers to be the result of natural processes of evolution, providing reformist social agendas with a set of theories drawn from the social sciences. How different can this use of "transformations of heaven" *(tianyan)* really be from the way that neo-Confucians used the categories of Heavenly Principle to provide support for their social thought?

Heavenly Principle and Universal Principle were used not only for critiques of society by gentry elites, for social protest by lower classes, as evidence for the legitimacy of an old order's replacement by a new order, or even as the ultimate moral goal of modern revolutions, but also as evidence for the legitimacy of ruling orders in different societies. A wide variety of critical movements and resistance movements understood Heavenly Principle or Universal Principle to be ultimate, universal values; by slicing through the artificial linkages between either Heavenly Principle or Universal Principle and the existing order, they exposed how essential aspects of that order were in conflict with Heavenly Principle or Universal Principle. Yet if this absolute and universal value were to become removed from the actual activities of resistance, it would, in turn, become a basis of legitimacy for a new set of hierarchical relations. In this sense, ideas such as Heavenly Principle and Universal Principle were similar to ancient ideas of the Mandate of Heaven *(tian ming)*: they used the name of heaven/nature *(tian)* or the universal *(gong)* to bring legitimacy to existing orders, and also used the name of heaven or the universal to provide a rational basis for revolution and rebellion. Modern society, therefore, did not extract itself from a dependence on a self-legitimating universal set of values, which is also to say that modern society never completely unified society's modes of existence with its modes of evaluating moral questions in the way that was achieved in the ancient society of rites/music.[6] The worldviews of Heavenly Principle and Universal Principle both appeal to daily life to discuss morality and questions of political legitimacy, but both also retain certain metaphysical characteristics and certain degrees of tension and distinction between the actual and the ideal. In this sense, the worldview of Universal Principle follows the logic of the worldview of Heavenly Principle to establish its own rationality and legitimacy.

Any understanding of Heavenly Principle or Universal Principle cannot and should not begin with a highly precise conceptual definition of the terms, but rather from a discussion of the processes of their historical emergence. The historical processes in which these principles emerged are found in the conditions where they are manifested in everyday practices, such as politics, ethics, and economy. Heavenly Principle or Universal Principle are not abstract concepts, definitions, or forms of discipline, but are something that humans faced every moment of every day and that they needed to make choices and decisions. Therefore, even though various schools of Confucianism and modern historians of intellectual history and philosophy have offered a great number of definitions of Heavenly Principle and Universal Principle, these definitions cannot provide or advance an essential understanding of them. In this sense, an understanding of the relationship between Heavenly Principle and Universal Principle cannot concern itself merely with conceptual continuity and discontinuity, but should analyze the fundamental social transformations that occurred during this process of substitution and succession. If we say that the dominant position of the worldview of Heavenly Principle was produced in the process of the historical formation and perfection of the Tang and Song dynasties, and that the worldview of Universal Principle is a precondition for the modern, programmatic legitimacy of the nation-state, then there will be no possibility whatsoever that our examination of Heavenly Principle and Universal Principle and their mutual relations will bypass a discussion of systemic social changes. The concepts of Heavenly Principle or Universal Principle, however, are always linked to the choices and judgments that people make in specific situations and in the practice of daily life, and thus we can only grasp the fundamental significance of these two concepts by understanding social relations as a process of ethical and moral choices. In a certain sense, at the core of the social imaginary is the imagination of the moral order: all social relations must be interpreted as a moral relationship. For example, the scientific worldview tends to understand ethical relations as a material relation (relations of interest and necessity), and thus uses a knowledge about nature and society (natural sciences, social sciences, and human sciences) to eliminate the mysterious aspects of these relations. On the other hand, the worldview of Heavenly Principle is the exact opposite: it tends to see all material relations or relationships of interest as a moral relation, the heart-mind/nature relation, or a metaphysical relation, and thus uses a moral knowledge (neo-Confucianism, studies of the classics, or history) to understand all varieties of actual relations. Therefore, science, social sciences, and human sciences should all be understood as moral knowledge, whereas forms of Confucian learning such as neo-Confucianism, studies of the classics, and traditional history should also be understood as knowledge of nature, material things, systems, and behaviors. The former sees "principle" as a "material" relation, whereas the latter sees "material" as a relation of "principle"; therefore any inquiry into "principle" must take an inquiry into "material" as its starting point, and any inquiry into the "material" must take an inquiry into "principle" as its starting point. The distinction between *li* (principle) and *wu* (things/the material) must be understood through a discussion of the emergence, transformation, and conditions of these two concepts. It is for just this reason that I place *li* and *wu,* these two ancient yet very young categories, at the center of the historical narrative; by tracing their genealogies, I show how the continuously changing historical relationships between knowledge, institutions, and moral judgment unfold.

How, then, are we to understand the relationship between the worldviews of Heavenly Principle and Universal Principle? Let us begin with the common understanding of the worldview of Heavenly Principle. Its establishment was of decisive significance for the formation of neo-Confucianism *(lixue)* and provided a central category around which major questions of Confucian learning were reorganized and developed. From the Yuan dynasty onward, Cheng-Zhu neo-Confucianism was established by rulers as the standard version of official Confucian learning. This political development led the neo-Confucian worldview to become a dominant ideology, to the extent that any practice of thought directed against the dynasty and its institutions would always to some degree constitute an implied critique of neo-Confucianism. Ming-dynasty "learning of the heart-mind" *(xinxue)* and "unadorned learning" *(puxue)* both implied a certain degree of rejection and resistance to official neo-Confucian learning. Such critiques of official neo-Confucianism, however, did not necessarily enable those versions of critical thought to escape the basic assumptions of neo-Confucianism. On this matter, two points merit special attention. First, a suitable distinction must be made between official neo-Confucianism and the neo-Confucianism of the gentry elites, thereby placing into a more complex set of historical relationships the processes by which a certain kind of neo-Confucianism gained official status and by which other critiques of dynastic institutions were presented by neo-Confucian thinkers. Second, forms of Confucian learning such as "learning of the heart-mind," "unadorned learning," and studies of history were all produced through rejection and critique of neo-Confucianism, especially official neo-Confucianism. However, these schools of thought retained to varying degrees some of the basic concerns of neo-Confucianism and continued to respond to some of the problems to which neo-Confucian thinkers also attempted to respond. Important themes in Qing-dynasty thought epitomized by Gu Yanwu's statement that "the study of principle *(lixue)* was the study of the classics *(jingxue)*" emphasized that the model of the study of the classics was the only appropriate path for answering those basic questions put forward by neo-Confucian learning, and thus forms of Confucian learning such as "learning of the heart-mind," studies of classics, and studies of history can all be seen as the transformation, development, and extension of the neo-Confucian worldview. Fundamental challenges to the neo-Confucian worldview did arrive in the late-Qing era: in the process of reforming state institutions, Universal Principle, a concept with a type of new, positivist-oriented view of science, rose to become the highest category that could provide the basis of rationality and legitimacy for politics, morality, and processes of recognition. With their position supported by this Universal Principle, reformist gentry and intellectuals used a new kind of scientific view of the universe and theories of society to undertake a thoroughgoing critique of the worldview of Heavenly Principle, ultimately supplanting it in terms of ideology and institutions of knowledge.[7]

The process by which the scientific worldview of Universal Principle established its hegemony can be divided into two distinct phases. In the late-Qing period, scientific thought, scientific practice, and scientific knowledge were an organic part of the larger body of social thought, social practice, and new knowledge. However, Yan Fu, Liang Qichao, Du Yaquan (1873–1933), and many other editors of and writers for scientific periodicals did not coalesce into a fully specialized scientific community. These figures' interpretations of the meaning of science, whether they were put forward by advocates for reform or propagandists for revolution, were always limited by the boundaries of rhetorical models such as science/civilization, science/historical era, science/state, or science/society. With the establishment of the Republic of China, specialized communities of science did form out of the division and growth of other social groups and knowledge communities, establishing their legitimacy through a position of specialization that was unrelated to politics, society, culture, and other such fields. This faith in science for science's sake was the product of a new division of labor and new institutions of knowledge. Why, then, did these professions of science and their practices in education and technical fields, which supposedly were unrelated to society and politics, form into such an authoritative force in the social-political field? Why was it that the strict division between science and humanistic knowledge led to the scientific view of the universe and the dominance of scientific discourse over fields of humanistic learning? If our discussion departs from the hegemonic position of worldview of Universal Principle and its methodology, we have no way to explain this phenomenon.

The concept of Universal Principle is closely related to the rise of modern European epistemology, became the foundation of modern European science and the methodologies of the human sciences. According to Gadamer,

> Modernity is defined—notwithstanding all disputed datings and derivations—quite univocally by the emergence of a new notion of science and method. This notion was worked out initially in a partial field of study by Galileo and philosophically grounded for the first time by Descartes. Since the seventeenth century, therefore, what we today call philosophy is found to be in a changed situation. It has come to need legitimation in the face of science in a way that had never been true before; and for all of two centuries right down to the death of Hegel and Schelling, it was actually constructed in such a self-defense against the sciences. The systematic edifices of the last two centuries are a dense succession of such efforts to reconcile the heritage of metaphysics with the spirit of modern science. Thereafter, with the entry into the positive age, as it has been called since Comte, one seeks to save oneself upon solid land from the storms of mutually conflicting world views with a merely academic seriousness about the scientific character of philosophy. And so philosophy entered into the bog of historicism, or got stranded in the shallows of epistemology, or goes back and forth in the backwater of logic.[8]

Working from a variety of perspectives and directions, thinkers such as Descartes, Hobbes, Locke, and Hume developed concepts of atomism and individualism into a systematic method for observing the world, replacing the central position of God with the central position of the human being. In this focus on the human as individual, the first question faced by modern European thought was the relationship between the person and his or her environment—material objects and other intelligences: How did humans understand people and things that were external to them? How did consciousness and knowledge of the world develop? What kinds of mechanisms controlled the ways that humans obtain knowledge? We understand these principles of epistemology to be the worldview of Universal Principle because, since the Enlightenment in eighteenth-century Europe, people have attempted to use these epistemological principles to discover the principles of the natural universe and a set of moral principles that are both rational and just. They have argued that these principles

> are equally valid and place equal restrictive power on all rational and reflective beings, regardless of the particularities of their cultural traditions, religious backgrounds, political orders, or moral and ethical structures. In politics, this ambition was expressed in the major declarations that emerged from the American Revolution and French Revolution. Among philosophers, Hume, Diderot, Bentham, and Kant all endeavored to provide theoretical explanations of these principles.[9]

The transformation from Heavenly Principle to Universal Principle is a process of extreme conflict. Just as the dominance of the Heavenly Principle worldview was produced through institutional relationships, the dominance of the Universal Principle worldview was produced through the establishment of the model of sovereignty of the modern state and its institutions of knowledge. If the worldview of Heavenly Principle used the order and institutions of rites as a natural and rational order, then the worldview of Universal Principle used atomism and individualism to deconstruct and critique the worldview of Heavenly Principle and its social significance.

Heavenly Principle and Universal Principle both address questions of the relationship between heart-mind *(xin)* and things *(wu)* and the order of things: "Heaven" *(tian)* and "Universal" *(gong)* both represent an appeal or claim to universality, whereas "Principle" *(li)* indicates a rule or law that both exceeds "things" yet is also internal to "things." It is worth noting that, during the process in which the worldview of Universal Principle put forward a sharp critique of the worldview of Heavenly Principle,

"principle" *(li)*, a concept that represents the universal order beyond time and space, was in fact retained, even in this revolutionary transformation. An obvious piece of evidence for this comes from the Chinese language itself: in Chinese, the concept of Heavenly Principle *(tianli)* and Universal Principle *(gongli)* both rely on and appeal to the concept of "principle" *(li)* and ideas behind it. Late-Qing intellectuals used categories such as "the study of principle" *(lixue)*, "fathoming patterns" *(qionglixue)*, "investigation of things" *(gewu)*, and "extension of knowledge" *(gezhi)* to translate the term "science" and its processes of understanding, thereby forming unintentional, unconscious linkages between Universal Principle—a concept from the natural sciences—and Heavenly Principle—a category from neo-Confucianism.[10] With these facts in mind, we cannot avoid the following questions: Why did both the ancient order and modern order need to appeal to the category of "principle" *(li)*? Why could category of "principle" *(li)* be used in modern epistemology? Just what kind of relationship exists between the worldview of Heavenly Principle and the Universal Principle (scientific) worldview? Is it a relationship of continuity or one of revolutionary supplantation? As with the development of neo-Confucianism, a process of institutionalization accompanied the development, spread, and transmission of the scientific worldview and its genealogy of knowledge. Therefore, in order to answer the questions just posed, we must analyze the process of the establishment of Heavenly Principle and its subsequent evolution. To understand the significance of Heavenly Principle, we must consider the following questions:

First, the concept of Heavenly Principle was produced in an environment of Confucian learning deeply influenced by the ideology of reviving antiquity *(fugu zhuyi)*. Beginning in the latter period of the Tang dynasty, Han Yu (768–824) and others declared that continuity with the Confucian orthodoxy *(daotong)* that stretched back to the time of Mencius (c. 371–c. 289 B.C.?) had been lost. This opinion was generally accepted by Confucian scholars of the Northern Song dynasty, who also took the restoration of orthodoxy as their duty. According to the worldview that advocated reviving antiquity, the Three Dynasties of Antiquity (Xia, Shang, and Zhou) *(sandai zhi zhi)* constituted the ideal society. In historical documents and political-moral discourses from this period, we

can repeatedly see a model of discourse that draws sharp contrasts between a variety of institutions from the Three Dynasties of Antiquity and
the Qin and Han dynasties—the distribution and division of land, the
organization of the military, the educational system, the state bureaucracy, and so forth. This model of discourse was produced by a consciousness of historical discontinuity. If we say that imaginings of the Three
Dynasties of Antiquity are an important factor or theme in Confucian
learning from Confucius onward, then it is also true that Song-dynasty
Confucian learning structured this imagination of the Three Dynasties
into a full consciousness of history and a critical resource. It is especially
worth noting that Heavenly Principle was produced not by a sense of
historical continuity, but rather was produced by a sense of historical *discontinuity,* and that the pursuit of Heavenly Principle itself must appeal
to the power of the subject, a kind of will that, through the subject's practice, re-creates historical continuity that has been broken. In this respect,
the sense of historical discontinuity has internal connections with the
production of agency *(zhutixing).* This sense of discontinuity bore a deep
and lasting influence on a wide variety of forms and developments of
Confucian learning—such as neo-Confucianism, studies of the classics,
and studies of history.

Let us begin our discussion with the relationship between a universal Heavenly Principle and the consciousness of a historical break or rupture. What must first be taken into consideration is the way in which this
sense of historical rupture was expressed: historical rupture expresses
not only the ending of a linear, unidirectional genealogy of orthodoxy
(daotong), but also the historical fragmentation between rites/music and
institutions, i.e., the institution of rites and music of the Three Dynasties
of Antiquity underwent a dissimulation in the process of historical
change, as in the case of the shift from a system of enfeoffment to a system of centralized administration, the shift from nonofficial schools and
academies to the civil examination system, the decline of the well-field
(jingtian) system and the rise of the equal-field *(juntian)* system, the sinicization of foreigners, China's conversion to foreign customs, etc.: these
changes were not a continuation of orthodoxy, but rather phenomena
produced *after* the break from orthodoxy. It was through the emergence

of this kind of historical consciousness that Song-dynasty Confucian scholars, through the development of interpretations of Heavenly Principle, were able to develop grounds for criticism and intervention in politics and everyday life. The concept of time put forward by the ideology of restoring antiquity—that is, historical "discontinuity," not "continuity"— provided an internal logic to the establishment of Heavenly Principle: Confucian scholars, then, had to establish connections with the Sage-Kings of antiquity through their discussion of Heavenly Principle and the Way of Heaven. Heavenly Principle was established in a discourse in which orthodoxy or the ideal order had already been cut off. Song-dynasty Confucians attempted to use this concept to establish a new understanding of the relationships between historical change and the ideal order or the natural order. Because the consciousness of rupture was expressed through the dissimulation between rites and music and institutions, heated debates surrounding Heavenly Principle and how to understand it were always closely tied to problems of political systems and daily life. It is exactly in this sense, then, that Heavenly Principle became the core of political-ethical consciousness for Confucian scholar-gentry from the Song dynasty onward.[11]

Second, by starting from the paradoxical relationship between Heavenly Principle and history, we can analyze the relationship between Heavenly Principle and "propensity of the times" *(shishi)*. Under conditions in which the rites and music of the Three Dynasties of Antiquity had dissolved or, put another way, under conditions in which actual institutions were unable to provide moral rationality, Heavenly Principle was structured into the ultimate criterion and basis for moral evaluation. Therefore, the only way to reconstruct historical continuity was to cleave to Heavenly Principle, and thus the investigation of it and the investigation of history were, in fact, the same process. However, in the conclusions reached by Song-dynasty Confucians, cleaving to Heavenly Principle was not equivalent to a return to the ideal political system of antiquity, and thus Heavenly Principle was not locked in the ideal past. Heavenly Principle was produced not only from within a sense of historical fragmentation, but also from within a state that faced toward the present and the future. Heavenly Principle existed within a "natural propensity of principle" *(ziran zhi lishi)* or "propensity of the times" *(shishi)*—and "propensity of the times" or "natural propensity of principle" became important internal aspects of Heavenly Principle.

"Propensity of the times" *(shishi)* is a concept used to transform historical rupture into continuity, as in the following line from Han Yu's "Rhyme-Prose of Taking Pity on Myself" *(Min ji fu):* "I regret that I cannot measure up to the men of ancient days; this is but the result of the propensity of the times."[12] In the *Emperor's Four Treasuries (Siku quanshu),* "propensity of the times" appears about 1,458 times, with 154 occurrences in texts related to the *Book of Changes (Yijing)* under the "classics" category *(jing bu),* with the majority of the remainder using the term to explicate the *Analects* and the *Mencius.* In the collections of texts by individual writers *(zi bu),* the term occurs 216 times, with many other instances in historical writings *(shi bu).* The *Analects* makes no reference to "propensity of the times," but Mencius praised Confucius as a "sage of timeliness" *(yi sheng zhi shi zhe),* which followed the commentary on the *gen* trigram in the *Book of Changes* that argues "rest when it is time to rest and move forward when it is time to move forward. When action and rest are not out of accord with the times, the Way is bright and clear."[13] Many subsequent commentators used the idea of "propensity of the times" or "propensity of principle" to explicate the *Analects* and *Mencius.* Cheng Yi (1033–1107) wrote: "To recognize the time and understand its [propensity], this is the great advice imparted by the study of the *Book of Changes.*"[14] Lu Zuqian (1137–1181) wrote: "To act in accordance with the purport of the times is great indeed. Men of the previous generation said that the 380 trigrams of the *Book of Changes* could be understood simply in terms of 'timeliness' *(shi).* Mencius grasped the indescribable greatness of Confucius by calling him 'a sage of timeliness.'"[15] To describe the principles of the *Book of Changes* in terms of "propensity of the times" was to make historical changes and their principles—as well as considerations on how to respond to these historical changes and their principles—into central problems of Confucian thought. Beginning with this view of the universe, Confucian thinking established an inherent link between the propensity of the times and moral action, emphasizing that "moral action *(dexing)* is quickened by the propensity of the times."[16] Confucian thinking also put forward the idea of the necessity for people to exercise power within an established framework, arguing the following:

> In the conduct of his affairs, the sage weighs *(quan)* what the situation requires and endeavors to begin at the proper time. Weighing what the situation requires is the guiding principle in all things, and action at the proper time is the leading principle in all affairs. Therefore there are few who, without relying on what the situation requires and in opposition to the propensity of the times, are able to carry a task to completion.[17]

In their use of principle *(li)* to explain Heaven *(tian)*, Song-dynasty Confucian scholars gradually came to replace the concept of "propensity of the times" with the concept of "propensity of principle" *(li shi)*, and thus the rhetoric of "adjustment to historical conditions" *(shishi)* came to provide a basis for interiority. In the works of Cheng Yi, we find only one mention of "propensity of the times" *(shi shi)*; in Zhang Dai's works, three mentions of "propensity of principle" *(li shi)*; in Zhu Xi's works, sixty-three uses of "propensity of the times" or "propensity of principle"; in the works of Lu Xiangshan, four uses of "propensity of the times" appear. Originally, the concept of "propensity of the times" was closely related to the *Yijing*, but Zhang Dai's work, *Hengqu's Discussions on the Book of Changes (Hengqu Yijing shuo)*, substituted "propensity of principle" with "propensity of the times," as in this statement: "As for when the propensity of principle changes, and one cannot fully match with the current times, then this is not the most advantageous route."[18] Zhu Xi used both "propensity of the times" and "propensity of principle," but the frequency of the use of "propensity of principle" was much higher. For example,

> All principle *(li)* under heaven is based in what is correct and without deviance. It begins in what flows and is without blockage. Therefore, in regard to all propensity under heaven, that which is correct and fluid is always heavy and need not rely on anything external; that which is deviant and runs in opposition is always light and must rely on assistance from others. This is the inevitable result of the propensity of principle *(lishi)*.[19]

"Propensity of the times" or "propensity of principle" relate to the significance of historical change: the function of these concepts is to explain why the institutions of the Sage-Kings of antiquity underwent transformations. It is very obvious that the concept of "propensity of the times" or "propensity of principle" were produced under conditions of historical rupture or disconnection from orthodoxy, and thus consciousness of historical rupture and consciousness of historical continuity exist side by side. Under conditions of historical rupture, "continuity" cannot be clearly delineated as specific historical instances of continuity, and thus continuity becomes a kind of internal, essential process and state; that is, continuity must make these delineations using abstract methods. Categories such as "time," "propensity," "propensity of the times," "propensity of principle," or "nature" *(ziran)* are all used in the midst of historical change to delineate and demonstrate the universal existence of the concept of Heavenly Principle. As historical change defines itself in terms of the dissimulation of the institutions of rites and music and strict divisions between the periods before and after the Three Dynasties period, then rupture becomes a part of the historical process, and people must ask: Just what force is dominating this historical process? How is it possible to grasp Heavenly Principle amidst continuous change or fragmentation? The concepts of "propensity of the times" or "propensity of principle" were produced in just this process of questioning. In the viewpoints produced by these two concepts, any effort to restore or return to the ideal conditions of the Three Dynasties must be based on a natural propensity of principle or propensity of the times, otherwise there is no way to understand why it is precisely the *discontinuity* that lies between the rites/music of the institutions of the Three Dynasties on the one hand and subsequent eras on the other that becomes the necessary form for constructing historical continuity. Mencius said that Confucius was "a sage of timeliness"; the *Book of Rites (Li ji)* says, "In (judging of) rites, the time should be the great consideration."[20] Here "time" and "timely" *(shi)* refers not only to an era and the changes it underwent but also to changes that take place through the propensity of the times. In the context of mainstream Confucianism, what is emphasized by "propensity" is a natural trend or natural force that dominates material changes: this natural trend or natural force certainly always takes effect through individuals, institutions, and events that push for its self-realization, but it cannot be equated with material processes in themselves. The transition from "propensity of the times" to "propensity of principle" implies a weakening of the significance of time: what is emphasized by the concept of "propensity of principle" is the interiority of propensity. The importance of the concepts of "propensity of the times" or "natural propensity of principle" lies in the fact that even as Confucian scholars provided a kind of political ideal based in the ideology of reviving antiquity, the political ideals of this revivalism could not be equated with a "fundamentalism" mired in the old doctrine of earlier Confucian thought.

During the Tang-Song period, the idea of propensity of the times was closely related to views on the natural development of history or natural occurrence of historical events; "propensity of the times" was opposed to the Han-dynasty view of the universe expressed in the "Mandate of Heaven." For example, Liu Zongyuan argued that the transformation of political institutions was a product of the propensity of the times or a product of "adjustment to historical conditions" *(shishi)* and rejected the idea that any one political system could claim to be absolutely rational. These arguments created a philosophy of history centered on political forms. Just as Hegel saw the family, civil society, and the state as forms of historical evolution, Liu Zongyuan saw the system of enfeoffment and system of centralized administration as results internal to historical change: the transitions from "the rise of the power of rulers and the administering of punishments" in the earliest societies to the "establishment of the various nobles," from the regional earls *(fangbo)* and aggregation leaders *(lianshuai)* in feudal states to the system of centralized administration with concentrated central power,[21] were the products of long processes of historical evolution. Liu Zongyuan's view of the propensity of the times was, on the one hand, a rejection of the Han-dynasty framework of "mutual correspondence between Heaven and Man" that justified permanent rule of the system of enfeoffment and, on the other hand, an argument for a system of centralized power. Unlike Hegel, however, Liu's argument did not rely on an appeal to a teleological view of history, but rather was established on the views of history and nature expressed by concepts such as "production and reproduction" *(shengsheng)* and "natural occurrence" *(zisheng)*, expressed first in the *Book of Changes* and the *Zhuangzi* and elaborated by Guo Xiang (?–312). Springing from views of history and nature represented by "production and reproduction" and "natural occurrence," the system of centralized power defended by Liu Zongyuan also did not possess an eternal rationality, but rather was the product of the constantly changing propensity of the times.[22] The idealist attitude toward the Three Dynasties held by neo-Confucian scholars such as Zhu Xi was in some ways different from Liu Zongyuan's view, but was identical to Liu's view in the way it explained the rationality of the institutions of subsequent dynasties in terms of propensity of the times or "propensity of principle in nature."

In the development of Confucian thought, especially neo-Confucian thought, propensity of the times or a consciousness of propensity of the times is a neglected yet extremely important topic; this concept has served a key function in at least two areas. First, the concept of propensity of the times places history and its changes into the category of nature, deconstructing the decisive role that the Mandate of Heaven played in the human realm, and providing a space for historical acts by the subject. From the view of historical evolution, the Three Dynasties, serving as a moral-political ideal, are in a position that is hidden and not visible to the outside; the ideal of the Three Dynasties exists amid the process of change, and exists in the decisions weighed and made at every minute and every hour, but is not found in preexisting doctrine or in the mechanical reproduction of these doctrines. Neo-Confucians use the concept of nature to distinguish between events *(shi)* and things *(wu)*, dividing all things between "natural" and "unnatural," judging what was natural and what was unnatural in terms of changes generated by the propensity of the times. Song-dynasty Confucian scholars frequently linked "investigating things and extending knowledge" with the concept of "knowing where to rest" *(zhi zhi)*.[23] In this instance, "to rest" is a criterion that lies between what is natural and what is unnatural and requires a subject *(zhuti)* in order to be grasped. Song-dynasty Confucians venerated the Three Dynasties but did not use specific policies from the Three Dynasties as a plan for practice, opting instead to uphold Heavenly Principle as a way both to seek out a rational solution in the midst of historical change and as a way to appeal to the goal of reaching sagehood through practice of individual self-cultivation in daily life. From recurring debates about "investigation of things" to sincere attempts to think through the relationship between accepted standards (*jing*) and expedients (*quan*), Song-dynasty Confucians and those who followed them all attempted to grasp the criteria of moral-political practice and the limits of propriety from within the framework of the movements of historical change, propensity of the times, or the natural propensity of principle. In his *Evidential Studies of the Meanings of Characters in the Mencius (Mengzi zi yi shu zheng)*, Dai Zhen (1724–1777) provided a distinction between the natural (*ziran*) and the necessary (*biran*), placing great importance on the concept of the "expedient" (*quan*): the "expedient" implies that the subject must balance decisions between Confucian principles and specific situations and environments, reaching a harmonious balance between nature, propensity of the times, and human relationships.[24] In the process of naturalizing history, the concept of "propensity of the times" played an important role; if Heavenly Principle exists within the propensity of the times, then the individual must make decisions according to his or her ability to cultivate the self and to evaluate the propensity of the times. In this sense, the synthesis between Heavenly Principle and propensity of the times is precisely what provides space for the practice of the subject.

Second, the concept of propensity of the times reorganizes fragmented histories into relationships of natural transformation, thereby also creating a historical subject of natural historical transformation. Otherwise, once history has become fragmented and discontinuous, how are people to be able to reorganize it into a genealogy of institutional change that takes the Three Dynasties as its starting point? Changes in relations among different ethnic groups, the changing of dynastic genealogies, shifts in social structures, radical change in language and customs—all of these can be seen within the changes of propensity of the times and can be placed within an endlessly rich set of transformations experienced by the historical subject. Therefore, this concept provided an essential framework of identification for a consciousness of community or for a Chinese identity. In neo-Confucianism or learning of the heart-mind *(xinxue)*, concepts such as the "natural propensity of principle" or "that which is made necessary by the propensity of principle" sought out the possibility of communication between Heavenly Principle and history. In the study of the classics and history, the concept of propensity of the times provided an important grounding for historical methodology: if Heavenly Principle existed within the propensity of the times, then it is a methodological error to pursue Heavenly Principle according to the methods of metaphysics—Heavenly Principle is a means of self-emergence for historical events, and any inquiry into Heavenly Principle that departs from historical change (like changes in customs and changes in political forms) will be unable to reach a true understanding of Heavenly Principle. Song neo-Confucianism *(lixue)* and classical studies *(jingxue)* together provided an important basis for Confucian views of history and methodology: neo-Confucianism placed moral practice within the order of the practice of self-cultivation, whereas classical studies argued that this process must be grounded in music and rites. Song- and Ming-dynasty neo-Confucianism and classical studies of the Qing dynasty all took the following questions as their basic points of departure: If deep discontinuity and transformation already separates the Three Dynasties from what followed, what must be done before we can reach a world that is truly in accord with rites and music? If we say that Song and Ming dynasty Confucian scholars thought through this question from within a framework of "investigating things and extending knowledge," then scholars of "unadorned learning" *(puxue)* attempted to use a unique methodology that would span all historical change, restoring every detail of a world governed by rites and music. Beginning with this question, Gu Yanwu developed an extremely precise set of methods of evidential learning, combining the methods of close textual investigation and phonology with an interest in historical developments, pursuing at each level the true sounds (of music) and significance (of rites) of the Three Dynasties according to their changes with the propensity of the times. According to Gu Yanwu's practices of phonology and philology and his discussions of customs and institutions, the internal threads of historical change formed the core of the methodology of evidential learning.[25] Zhang Xuecheng's famous dictum that "the Six Classics are all history" not only provided an understanding of the contents of the classics, but also made the historical conditions of the formation of the classics as well as the changes they underwent an essential part of any understanding of the classics. In his argument that the *Dao* and actual things and affairs were unitary *(dao qi yi ti)*, Zhang made the knowledge of the sages subordinate to the processes of "nature" themselves.[26] The knowledge of the sages, in his view, was a knowledge of "what could not but be the case," knowledge that was produced through insightful observations of nature. Beginning with this historical ontology, Zhang developed a way of explaining the *Dao* through the relationships between historical changes to the system of rites/music and, from the relationships found in the propensity of the times, developed a critique of classifications of knowledge such as the "Six Arts" *(liu yi)*, "Seven Summaries" *(qi lue)*, and "Four Categories of Literature" *(si bu)* and their significance. When seen in terms of the transformation of the propensity of the times, the relationship between classic *(jing)*/master *(zi)* and classic *(jing)*/biography *(zhuan)* has been thoroughly upended: the master and biography are no longer produced through an understanding of "classics" *(jing)*, but the classics are produced in the way that they are restructured by masters and biographies; in other words, the father does not produce a son, but the son produces the father. This process of structuring the classics is in itself a product of institutional transformation (such as the establishment of the system of erudites [*boshi*] by Qin and Han scholars). In this respect the idea of propensity of the times provided a foundation for the birth of an archaeology and genealogy of the classics. For an archaeology or genealogy of the classics, the center of inquiry now includes not only exegesis of and evidential scholarship on the texts of the classics, but also an inquiry into the relationship between the process by which the classics obtain meaning and significance and their relationship to the propensity of the times—in other words, the politics and historicity of classical learning. From the standpoint of this particular kind of classical learning, both Gu Yanwu and Zhang Xuecheng understood the Three Dynasties of Antiquity and their institutions of rites/music to be the source of an ideal morality and politics, and both men strove to develop a complete set of methods similar to that of the rule of the Three Dynasties of Antiquity. It was precisely because of this understanding of the propensity of the times that they structured their political-moral ideal in a way that avoided fundamentalism. Both Gu Yanwu's call to "suffuse the spirit of the system of enfeoffment within the system of centralized administration" *(yu fengjian yu junxian)* and Zhang Xuecheng's discussion of establishing a method of historiography from within historical changes were based on the Confucian view of the propensity of the times.[27]

By bringing together three major themes of neo-Confucianism such as the rule of the Three Dynasties of Antiquity, the propensity of the times (history) and Heavenly Principle, we can then understand why "investigation of things and extension of knowledge" *(gewu zhi zhi)* from the Song dynasty onward became such an important point of debate among Confucian scholars. The reference to and inspiration provided by the Three Dynasties of Antiquity was produced by a sense of historical rupture; and, when seen in terms of changes in the propensity of the times, this rupture served in various ways as an expression of the dissimulation between rites/music and institutions. In formulations of neo-Confucianism and historiography, the problem of the separation between rites/music and institutions was produced by an understanding of the distinction between the rites/music of antiquity and actual institutions. In other words, the rites/music of antiquity, which once could express the will of Heaven and standards of morality, had already transformed through course of history into a functionalist institution that was unable to commune with the will of Heaven. Separation between rites/music and institutions, however, was the result of transformations in propensity of the times, and the propensity of the times in itself was a means of expression for Heaven. Therefore, even if the institutions, customs, scholarship, and other practices of later dynasties were already completely detached from the rites and music of antiquity, as phenomena produced by transformations of propensity of the times, they still serve as "traces" that express and communicate ideal knowledge or the will of the sages. Seen in this light, in one sense, neither existing systems, laws, standards, nor orders that appeal to the words of the sages, nor knowledge passed down by our forebears, nor the authority of lords and kings can be equated with the rites and music of the Sage-Kings or with a universal Heavenly Principle;

this concept of Heavenly Principle (as well as the binary between rites/ music and institutions) constitutes a type of questioning or suspicion of institutional authority. In another sense, any investigation of Heavenly Principle is inevitably an investigation of actually existing institutions, customs, habits, and scholarship. The pursuit of Heavenly Principle is a process that emerges from the interplay of general Confucian principles and specific historical situations, and thus many people became concerned with the question of what kind of method, path, and process can be used to discover, experience, or show Heavenly Principle within the transformation of propensity of the times. If we say that a sense of rupture or separation from orthodoxy fueled the desire to restructure a sense of continuity with that orthodoxy through individual self-cultivation and political practice, then the concept the propensity of the times also drove the need for a strong and robust methodology: What method could connect "things" and their changes, which are always tied to specific circumstances, while also obtaining an understanding of the general order? What method can overcome the externality and temporariness of "things" (*wu*) and reach a unity with "principle" (*li*)?

These questions are the internal force that led "investigating things and extending knowledge" (*gewu zhi zhi*) to become a major point of contention in debates among Confucian scholars from the Song dynasty onward. The paradox of "investigating things and extending knowledge" can be described as follows. On the one hand, if one lacks an understanding of Heavenly Principle, then the appropriateness or validity of any form of daily life is open to question, and it is impossible to establish any understanding of the significance of forms of daily life. On the other hand, Heavenly Principle is internal to the process of the emergence of daily life itself, and thus any approach that treats "investigating things and extending knowledge" as a cognitive activity that is external to the practice of daily life will fail to grasp Heavenly Principle. Heavenly Principle is neither a product of "investigating things and extending knowledge" nor the creation of the sages, but rather an existence waiting to be discovered that is internal to daily life yet not the same as daily reality. From the perspective of Confucian learning, forms of daily life that accord with Heavenly Principle exist only under conditions set out by rites and music; if rites and music should devolve into hollow forms or merely functional institutions, then the relationship between Heavenly Principle and the everyday *Lebenswelt* is no longer transparent or direct, and thus it is only through the practice of "investigating things and extending knowledge" that one is able to reestablish internal connections between daily life and Heavenly Principle. In this sense, the demands placed by Confucian learning on methodology are deeply rooted in Confucian views of history. According to the historical perspective that is based on the separation of rites/music and institutions, the category of "things" *(wu)* has undergone deep transformation. In the category of pre-Qin rites and music, "things" are both a manifestation of the moral order and moral behavior in itself (the identical relation between "things" [*wu*] and "events" [*shi*] is established in the significance of the practices of rites and music), and thus the concept of "things" is identical to the concept of standards or norms; because the will of Heaven is directly manifested as the order of rites and music, the "things" as expressed in the "hundred things" *(bai wu)* within this order are also closely related to the idea of a natural order. However, with the separation between rites/music and institutions, the relationship between the will of Heaven and institutions becomes uncomfortable and unclear, and the normative meaning of "things" as understood in the discourse of rites and music gradually dissolves, and thus a concept of "things" appears that is unrelated to moral standards and focuses largely on the objectivity of representations (similar to the modern sense of the "fact"). Under conditions of dissimulation of rites/music and institutions, even if what is expressed by "things" are still the "events" found in the practice of ritual, because the practice of ritual in itself is formalistic and hollowed out, these practices, behaviors, and processes do not carry the significance of morality or standards of propriety. However, the shift in "things" took place in its relationship with the propensity of things, and thus possesses a dual nature: on the one hand, the shift in "things" is the result of fragmentation between rites/music and institutions, and thus "things" can no longer be equated with the standards of propriety within rites and music. On the other hand, if this process of fragmentation is a product of the propensity of the times, then the shift in "things" in itself is also a part of a natural process, and thus must hold the "traces" of Heavenly Principle. For these reasons, then, the methodology of "fathoming the principles of things and affairs" (*ji wu qiong li*) becomes a pathway to return to the world of rites/music or the world of Heavenly Principle under conditions created by changes that occur in the propensity of the times. In the senses described previously, the concept of "things" (facts), which stands in contrast to values or standards of propriety, is the product of the continued fragmentation of rites/music and the institutional order.[28] Debates in Song-Ming neo-Confucianism about whether "nature is principle" (*xing ji li*) and whether "the heart-mind is principle" (*xin ji li*) and Qing-dynasty scholars' critiques of neo-Confucianism are always related to this transformation of the category of "things": If "things" transformed into a category of "facts," then how could an inquiry into "things" or "the nature of things" (*wuxing*) yield a basis for moral practice? Are "things" the "ten thousand things" (*wanwu*), or "the heart-mind" (*ci wu*), or the standards that arise from the institutions of rites and music?

In Chinese thought, "principle" (*li*) is a freighted expression for ideas of order. At its core, the question of "principle" and "things" is a question of the relationship between stasis and change, continuity and discontinuity; it can also be said to be a question of how to understand a variety of historical relationships and their transformations as a rational and natural process. It is an extremely important thread in research on intellectual history. In the field of Chinese thought, the concept of "principle" (*li*) is linked with categories such as "the Way" (*dao*), "matter-energy" (*qi*), "nature" (*xing*), the "heart-mind" (*xin*), "things" (*wu*), "names" (*ming*), and "words" (*yan*, also translated as "speech"). But "principle" obviously holds a central position in the logic of these categories: it combines and unites the common order and the transcendental order, the logic of cycles and the logic of linear change, thus becoming an omnipresent and natural category. What is meant by "omnipresent" is that "principle" is internal to the uniqueness of things and events; what is meant by "natural" is that "principle" is not a kind of rigid rule, but is an internal order that is expressed in the process of the transformation of "things" (*wu*). Any understanding of "principle" is always linked with the sense of uniqueness implied by the concept of "things." "Things" can refer to events and objects, and can also be ethical laws, objectively defined objects, subjective spirit, nature in its purity, and the practices of people.[29] From the perspective of "principle," the process of recognizing "things" always includes universalist assumptions about "principle"; yet from the perspective of "things," these assumptions about the universality of "principle" are always effected through specific situations and environments. Regardless of how the pursuit of practices of knowledge concerning "things" may become distant from our common understanding of moral behavior, it always has moral and ethical applications—at the same time, this judgment also implies that moral judgments and moral practices have always been moral judgments or moral practices that arise from specific situations and environments or relationships.

2. HEAVENLY PRINCIPLE AND UNIVERSAL PRINCIPLE

Since the late Qing, Chinese thought, institutions, and genealogies of knowledge have undergone extremely important transformations. Beginning with that period, scholars of various schools began to seek out the historical sources of this "modern" transformation. Just as many people are accustomed to seeing humanism (liberation from theocracy, gaining equality from feudal aristocracy, and establishing the central role of humans through the control of nature) as a central value of modernity, many people also understand the intellectual transformations that occurred in the Ming-Qing transition to be important historical clues for the appearance of modernity in China. Sharp differences can be found between the views on history presented by Liang Qichao, Hu Shi, and Hou Wailu, but their research on intellectual history shares two key judgments. The first key judgment is found in the argument that the turn in Song-Ming neo-Confucianism toward the modern can be found in the central place allotted to the "heart-mind" (*xin*) in the works of followers of Wang Yangming such as Wang Ji (1498–1583) and members of the Taizhou school such as Wang Gen (1483–1541). The most complete expression of this new view of order was put forward in the work of Li Zhi (1527–1602), who affirmed desire and self-interest. Modern scholars' arguments about the importance of the notions of the heart-mind in the Song and Ming dynasties clearly emerge from two frames of reference: first, the rise of ideas of the individual and the self in modern European thought; and second, modern thinkers' sharp critiques of neo-Confucianism and its social foundations. The second key judgment is found in arguments made by Liang, Hu, and Hou that the rise of evidential learning during the Qing dynasty contained positivist scientific methods and a teleological view of knowledge for the sake of knowledge. This revolution in methodology and views about the nature of knowledge were not only an attempt to resist "learning of the heart-mind and nature" *(xin xing lun)*, but also contained elements of modern scientific methods. This argument emerges from the dual background of modern European scientific thought and Chinese critiques of neo-Confucianism. These two fundamental viewpoints shared by Liang, Hu, and Hou established the basic context for understanding changes in Song-Ming neo-Confucianism and Qing-dynasty thought: the idea of the self (and new ideas about privacy) and positivist methods continuously broke through the limitations of the metaphysical idea of Heavenly Principle, providing an internal force for movement toward the modern in Chinese thought. According to this line of argument, the rise of modern thought can be described as follows: (1) the liberation of the human, the discovery of the self, and the establishment of equal rights among private individuals; and (2) the use of the power of science to drive out evil spirits, or a process of rationalization. According to this logic, we can also make the following argument: modern ideas of equality and modern ideas of science (which are, in a certain sense, completely identical) disavowed the existence of any innate hierarchies and attempted to remake society according to a scientific Universal Principle, and thus argued that a completely antithetical relationship existed between modern Universal Principle and Heavenly Principle, which attempted to naturalize traditional hierarchical relations. These two fundamental ideas together implied a substitution of natural philosophies: modern society no longer needed naturalistic categories such as Heaven or Heavenly Principle to serve as the basis of its legitimacy. In this sense, Heavenly Principle was incompatible with modern society, and the rise of the modern worldview coincided with its decline.

We must reexamine these two views of the rise of modern thought. First, the arguments described previously are all based on judgments that disavow neo-Confucianism; that is, all work in a direction opposed to neo-Confucianism to delineate modern elements within Chinese thought—as when, starting from the perspective of modern individualism, neo-Confucianism is seen as the ideology of the feudal hierarchies, or, when, starting from the perspective of positivist views of science, neo-Confucianism is defined as a metaphysics lacking any grounding in reality. The forms of Confucian thought clearly had undergone many changes: from arguments made by Zhu Xi that "nature is principle" *(xing ji li)* to Wang Yangming's statement that "the heart-mind is principle" *(xin ji li);* from the claims of the later adherents of the Wang Yangming (1472–1529) school that "there is no distinction of good and evil in the original substance of the mind"[30] to the argument made by Li Zhi (1527–1602) that there was "no other and no self" *(wu ren wu ji);* and from arguments made by Gu Yanwu and Huang Zongxi (1610–1695) for the virtue of self-interest to Sun Yat-sen's motto that "all under heaven is shared by all" *(tianxia wei gong).* All such changes, however, still took place from within the categories of Confucianism or contained internal elements of Confucian thought, and shared a view of order established by neo-Confucianism. These critical modes of thought exposed hierarchies/control relationships hidden beneath the robes of Heavenly Principle, but the basis on which they depended to critique and expose these relationships still lay within Heavenly Principle itself—a new understanding and interpretation of Heavenly Principle. For example, investigations into heart-mind, nature, and self undertaken by Wang Yangming and his disciples developed out of the basic assumptions of neo-Confucianism. Its critique of Cheng-Zhu neo-Confucianism can in itself be seen as a result of the internal fragmentation of neo-Confucianism. Both in terms of their intellectual direction and methodologies, studies of the classics and history from the early Qing inherited the tradition of "investigating things and extending knowledge" advocated by neo-Confucianism. At the same time, these fields attempted to use the classics and history to answer the basic questions put forward by neo-Confucianism. Huang Zongxi's thought on political institutions, Gu Yanwu's analysis of customs and habits, and Dai

Zhen's exposure of the way some could "kill people in the name of principle *(li)*"—all of these developments took place within categories internal to Confucian learning, and all were motivated by the desire to restore and establish the original meanings of Heavenly Principle and the Way of Heaven. Therefore, if one wishes to show definitively that late-Ming and early-Qing thought contained elements of modernity, then one must also ask whether neo-Confucianism itself also contained these elements; this question cannot be fully grasped within the framework of neo-Confucianism and anti-neo-Confucianism. The Northern and Southern Song dynasties substituted views of Heaven that had been dominant since the Han dynasty with the concept of Heavenly Principle, and saw it as a realm that every person could reach through self-cultivation and cognition. This transformation could only be accepted under the conditions of social change that took place during the Tang and Song dynasties, which were epitomized by the decline of the system of hereditary aristocracy. Internal linkages, then, were established between Heavenly Principle and the moral practices of individual subjects. From this historical perspective, if we only take the decline of the concepts of Heaven or Principle as indications of modernity, then we have no way to understand the complex historical relationships between "modern thought" or "elements of modern thought" and the worldview of Heavenly Principle.

Second, scholars' discoveries of elements of modernity in Ming-Qing thought or in "early enlightenment" thought *(zaoqi qimeng zhuyi)* are rooted in practices of social history that link an emphasis on the individual or the self and ideas of equality with the history of the development of capitalism. This view is a result of attempts to link the teleology of modernity to the development of capitalist relations. The disavowal of hierarchies or a focus on interiority are not, however, exclusively modern phenomena; we need to understand *which* hierarchy is being disavowed. For example, in the Wei-Jin period the concept of "principle" underwent an important transformation: following the expansion of the system of centralized administration during the Qin and Han dynasties, forms of thought emerged that reaffirmed the aristocratic system of hierarchies and limitations on the emperor's power. Ideas about "principle" held by important figures in the Wei-Jin period and their emphasis on reverence for the individual, self, and nature showed internal linkages to a desire to revive the spirit of the ancient system of enfeoffment that had emerged during a time of shared power between the imperial regime and powerful families *(menfa)*. Contrary to these developments, following the rebellion led by Wang Anshi during the Tang dynasty, people were deeply affected by the splitting up and loss of territory and crises created by war, and began to rethink questions of the necessity of maintaining a system that concentrated power in the hands of the emperor. Liu Zongyuan's essay "On Enfeoffment" *(Fengjian lun)* discussed the decline of the system of enfeoffment and the rise of social fluidity, mustering the "Way of Great Centrality" *(da zhong zhi dao)* against the system of official ranks *(pinji)*. The essay's argument for a grand unification of governance was closely related to the conflicts that arose between the Tang dynasty's expanding system of centralized administration and the older aristocratic hierarchies. The growth to maturity during the Northern and Southern Song dynasties of the civil examination system, the two-tax system *(liang shui fa)*,[31] and official bureaucratic system provided the basis for centralized political power and the development of urban economies, which, in turn, led to the total breakup of the aristocratic system characterized by enfeoffment. Set against this background, Song-dynasty Confucian scholars transformed "principle" and Heavenly Principle into foundational concepts of morality, setting them as a balance against the various institutions of the centralized administrative state and its standards; these scholars' concept of Heavenly Principle cloaked demands for shared power in the rhetoric of reviving antiquity. Based on their overall direction, we can see that the concept of Heavenly Principle was completely different from Liu Zongyuan's idea of the Way of Heaven (or the "Way of Great Centrality"), a politically freighted idea that he had used to attack the system of official rank and to establish a system of imperial power centered on the emperor. In fact, the problems emphasized by Heavenly Principle were how to place limitations on and balance out imperial power and the system of centralized administration. Therefore, on the one hand the emergence of the concept of Heavenly Principle shows an internal historical relation to the bankruptcy of hierarchies handed down from antiquity. On the other hand, this form of egalitarianism cannot be equated with a complete endorsement of new social relations that arose under conditions created by the system of centralized administration. For example, Song-dynasty Confucians used the well-field system (*jingtian zhi*) to resist the equal-field system (*juntian zhi*) and two-tax system, used the patriarchal clan system to resist institutions of bureaucratic administration, and used the idea of academies (*xuexiao*) to resist the imperial examination system. Song Confucians, then, would find the way modern people link social change with a teleological view of time to be quite foreign: their criterion for evaluating change was not time, but rather an internal criterion—"the propensity of principle" *(lishi)*.

Third, because the patriarchal clan system of the Ming-Qing era used the worldview of Heavenly Principle as the basis for justifying its legitimacy, the critique of the patriarchal clan system and its ideology presented by the New Culture and May Fourth movements placed the values of the individual and the self in opposition to the worldview of Heavenly Principle, working within a framework of egalitarianism to define the worldview of Heavenly Principle as the ideology of hierarchy. This rhetorical strategy concealed the historical relationship between modern egalitarianism and new forms of social hierarchy. The atomistic view of the individual is a legal abstraction set against the backdrop of the modern state system; this abstraction extracts people from relations of family and locality and other social relations to structure them as individual entities bound by duties and obligations. This legal abstraction does not vacate actual relations among people, but demands the use of a new model for actual relations to regulate individual behavior, thereby reorganizing society according to these new standards. When legal relations are unable to regulate people's behavior completely, the idea of the individual produces a kind of interior concept of the self, one that understands the individual as an entity with internal depth. This depth of the individual, in turn, becomes the basis of morality and sentiment. These are the background conditions for the production of self-discipline through morality and sentiment. An internal tension exists between the atomized individual and the category of the self, as the concept of the self produces resistance to individualist social institutions. The rise of modern society, then, is a systemic transformation, one that involves not only certain kinds of modes of recognition or individual rights and powers, but also a transformation of the entire social system and the basis of its legitimacy.

Fourth, it is on this point that we can find certain similar structures shared by the socially constructed oppositions that lie between the world-views of Heavenly Principle and Universal Principle. First, both ideas appeal to the value of equality. As they do so, however, they also serve to justify the legitimacy of projects to remake various social hierarchies. Second, certain connections exist between the modern concept of the self and ideas of the self found in neo-Confucianism and the "theory of the heart-mind and nature" *(xin xing lun)* found in "learning of the heart-mind" *(xinxue)*. In their varying discourses, they all give rise to certain kinds of resistance and to critiques of new forms of social relations. In other words, the worldviews of Heavenly Principle and Universal Princi-ple accept new forms of social change (such as the decline of the system of hereditary aristocracy and the rise of the new state system, etc.) as a historical premise, and thus lend themselves to an affirmation of new so-cial changes ("the propensity of the times"); both ideas, however, also contain internal tensions with these social changes and their legitimacy. For this reason, then, both principles also formed into critical intellectual resources for their respective eras. Heavenly Principle and Universal Principle are both internal to their respective eras but are also Others *(tazhe)* of their respective eras. It is this final point that distinguishes my narrative of Song-Ming neo-Confucianism from those views held by Naitō Konan and Miyazaki Ichisada: the Kyoto School's positive view of the Song dynasty is conditioned by assumptions about the nation-state. Their view of neo-Confucianism and its relation to elements of "Song-dynasty capitalism"—such as well-developed transportation, prosperous urban centers, a relatively free market, new systems of currency and taxa-tion, constantly evolving divisions of labor, bureaucratic institutions and efforts to expand education based on the civil examination system, and a growing separation between government and the military—was fully in concert with the ideology of "nationalism,"[32] and thus failed to discover the tensions and critical oppositions that lie between the worldview of neo-Confucianism and the social processes that are subsumed beneath the category of "Song-dynasty capitalism." It is essential, therefore, to distinguish between what Song-dynasty Confucians recognized as "the propensity of principle" *(lishi)* and those historical elements that today are included within such categories as modernity and capitalism; only then can we liberate these "key factors" from the logic of historical determinism (with modernization theory as the most complete and influential expression of this determinism in historical narrative). It is precisely this distinction that will be of great use to us in reaching a new understanding of the question of "the rise of modern Chinese thought": Why is it that we can see a type of paradoxical mode of thought, one that, to varying degrees, in the process of the pursuit of modernity, nonetheless retains critical stances toward capitalism and its political forms? This mode of thought can be found in the works of people such as Kang Youwei, Liang Qichao, Yan Fu, Zhang Taiyan, and Lu Xun (and in the leaders of two modern Chinese revolutions, Sun Yat-sen and Mao Zedong). How should we understand the complex relationships between modern thought and intellectual traditions from the Song dynasty onwards? Without a sense of the criteria and experiences that were part of these historical transitions, we have no way to understand the means by which they could both embrace and resist historical change, and we have no way to understand how they both pursued Universal Principle and firmly rejected declarations of universality that were made by borrowing the authority of Universal Principle.

Fifth, the worldviews of Heavenly Principle and Universal Principle all appeal to categories of the "natural" *(ziran)* and the "necessary" *(biran)* to justify the rationality of moral-political practice. Because they make distinctions between the natural and necessary, the natural and the unnatural, the necessary and the accidental, these two worldviews both give a central place to considerations of methodology. The former sees "investigating things and extending knowledge" as the sole path to reaching Heavenly Principle, whereas the latter sees the methods of science as the one and only way to understand Universal Principle. The worldviews of Heavenly Principle and Universal Principle both revolve around an absolute essence (*juedui cunzai*) that is both universal and internal (i.e., Heavenly Principle and Universal Principle), demolishing worldviews that combine moral judgment with specific backgrounds or conditions, such as the worldview of rites/music. The internal contradictions within the idea of "principle" *(li)* and the forces that lead to shifts within it are mainly expressed in two ways. First among these is the opposition between principle *(li)* and the methodology of the pursuit of principle *(li)*. Regardless of whether it is within the worldview of Heavenly Principle or in the worldview of Universal Principle, "principle" is a concept that extends through cosmology, metaphysics, and the "theory of the heart-mind and nature" *(xin xing lun)*. Incommensurable parts, however, always exist in the relationships between these different fields. As a metaphysical assumption (or faith), "principle" is something that is not concrete; as a cosmological assumption, it is something that can be thought; and as a kind of ethical order, it must be something that can be grasped through everyday practice. On the one hand, a general "principle" *(li)* assumed it had a route by which it would return into itself through specific practices of cognition and self-cultivation, thereby structuring a connection between the concept of Heavenly Principle and a positivist mode of "investigating things and extending knowledge" or scientific methodology. However, if the self-cultivation practices of "investigation of things and extending knowledge" gradually came to be understood as a methodology with empiricist aspects, then the moral implications of "investigation of things and extending knowledge" would transform into a practice of cognition of the world, thus demoting "principle" to a the role of objective rule or fact. On the other hand, "principle" *(li)* assumes an inherent interrelatedness between Heaven (Nature) and humans, and thus moral practice provides the precondition for the theory of the heart-mind and nature. According to the logic of the theory of the heart-mind and nature, "principle" is not an external object, and thus "investigating things and extending knowledge" should be understood as an activity or function that is inherent in the spirit *(xinling)* itself, and should not be confused with objective cognition of the world. Those ways of understanding that see "fathoming the principles of things and affairs" *(ji wu qiong li)* or scientific methods as the process of separating things and events into categories would simply be a distortion of "principle."

Moreover, a paradoxical relationship exists between Heavenly Principle and institutions. As a transcendent concept, "principle" contains the connections between individuals and Heavenly Principle, which is to say that every person can reach Heavenly Principle through everyday moral practice, and thus "principle" expresses a force and appeal that transcends specific power relations and institutions. Yet the concept of "principle" always draws on an idea of order (such as the institutions of rites/music or legal systems) for its inherent power, attempting to establish at another level a unified relationship between morality and existing institutions. An indivisible relationship exists, then, between "principle" and political or social order. The paradoxical relationship between "principle" and institutions can be described as follows: first, "principle" establishes itself on the dual foundation of the Way of Heaven or operations of nature and the cognition of the subject, attempting to use moral-political judgment as a basis to free itself from the control of dominant institutions and their systems of judgment, thus structuring a self-negation into the very idea of order assumed by "principle" that attempts to unify the ideal and the actual. Second, to overcome arbitrary and overly individual interpretations of "principle," people emphasize the objectivity of methodology, thereby creating a gulf between "knowledge" and practice that is difficult to bridge. The two problems just described are inherent in the concept of "principle" and the internal processes of its application. For this reason, then, methodology is something that is inherently needed by the worldviews of Heavenly Principle and Universal Principle but is also the force that causes crises to occur within the worldviews of Heavenly Principle and Universal Principle and leads them to break down under their own weight.

The difficulties inherent in the worldviews of Heavenly Principle and Universal Principle paved the way for three different intellectual orientations. The first was expressed as the self-negating tendencies within neo-Confucianism (*lixue*) and the orientations toward antihumanism inherent within modern thought: doubts about the relationship between Heavenly Principle and the methodology of "investigating things and extending knowledge to the utmost" within neo-Confucianism led to efforts to further internalize "principle," that is, linking principle (*li*) and the original mind-heart (*benxin*), the heart-mind (*xin*), the substance of quiescence (*jiti*), and nothingness, rejecting the idea that any project of knowledge or its institutionalization could provide a basis for moral practice. In essence, the transition from the substance of the moral mind (*xinti*) and the substance of the moral nature (*xingti*) to the substance of quiescence (*jiti*) and nothingness was also a process of moving from the person and his or her interiority to the self-negation of the person and his or her interiority. This logic, which develops interiority to its furthest extreme, is also a complete rejection of discourses on "investigation of things and extending knowledge" that contain any substantive epistemological project. A very similar logic appears in modern thought: for example, Zhang Taiyan brought together the ideas of Zhuangzi's "On Equalizing Things" (*Qiwu lun*), "consciousness-only" Yōgacāra Buddhism, and the philosophy of Friedrich Nietzsche to launch a fierce critique of notions of Universal Principle, evolution, and scientism, ultimately formulating a view of nature based in the equalization of all things to reject anthropocentric cosmologies and worldviews. The second orientation is found in new discourses on institutions that are internal to neo-Confucianism and also found in modern thought. The worldviews of Heavenly Principle and Universal Principle both assumed that a kind of ideal society (the Three Dynasties of Antiquity or the world of rites/music, the society of the future, or the world of *Da tong*, or Great Unity) could serve as a basis for moral-political practice, and thus also assumed a tense relationship between the ideal society and the actual world. The unity between humans and Heavenly Principle contained a systemic teleology, in which Heavenly Principle manifested itself in a kind of perfect combination or union between moral-political practice and an ideal order. From within this moral-political practice that was oriented toward Heavenly Principle, a kind of institutional argument was produced: any practice that did not rely on institutions or ritual had no way of reaching the moral goals set out by Heavenly Principle. A wide variety of thinkers placed institutional considerations at the center of their thinking, leading to the disintegration of views on the interiority of Heavenly Principle. These efforts ranged from work by neo-Confucian scholars to revive the practices of the patriarchal clan system and the well-field system to efforts by later adherents of the Wang Yangming school to dress and carry out rites in the style of Confucius; and from attempts to use the decrees and regulations of antiquity to imagine political-economic institutions (such as Huang Zongxi) to attempts to use the categories of "investigating things" to revive the practices of the classical Six Arts *(liu yi)* (such as Yan Yuan [1635–1704] and Li Gong [1659–1733]). This mode of thinking that tied Heavenly Principle closely with institutions also provided a basis for modern utopianism: both Kang Youwei's imaginations of future societies in *The Book of Great Unity (Da tong shu)* and the future world that was rooted in the socialists' rejection of the real world as it existed attempted to transform Heavenly Principle or Universal Principle from a state within the interior of the self into real-world institutions and to provide a basis for moral-political practice. Within this new institutional framework, the adversarial relationship between Heavenly Principle/Universal Principle and actual institutions was transformed into an adversarial relationship between different types of institutions. The third orientation can be found in new discourses on rites/music or debates on customs internal to Confucian learning and in neoclassicism *(xin gudian zhuyi)* in modern thought. As with the discourse on new institutions, the discourse on new rites/music and neoclassicism rejected abstract speculation and excessive internalization of Heavenly Principle, and saw the worldviews of Heavenly Principle/Universal Principle in themselves as a sign of the crisis of modernity. They resolutely maintained that moral-political practice must be established on real relationships of rites/music or institutional relationships. However, unlike discourses on new institutions, new discourses on rites/music or neoclassicism emphasized that institutions of rites/music are the products of tradition and its evolution, and that any discussions and moral-political practices that depart from customs, habits, language, and tradition will never be able to achieve a unity with Heavenly Principle. New rites/music discourses and neoclassicism contained two types of attitudes. The first was radical, using classical ideals to attack existing institutions, working to reconstruct forms of rites/music and classical institutions within their historical context, and basing the practices of reform on these efforts. The second, however, was conservative, emphasizing the evolution of rites/music and classical regulations, insisting that no moral-political practice could divert from rites/music, customs, habits, and the process of their evolution, and rejecting any mode of thought that attempted to imagine the future by diverging from these processes of change in themselves.

The three orientations just described present different aspects of contradictions that lie within the worldviews of Heavenly Principle/Universal Principle. At the same time, however, they are also predicated on three different views of Heavenly Principle/Nature. The first of these defines Nature/Heavenly Principle through the antithetical relationship between human action and Nature (Heavenly Principle). The second defines Nature/Heavenly Principle through the relationship between nature and necessity. Finally, the third defines Nature/Heavenly Principle through the relationship between Nature and the propensity of the times. These three views of Nature/Heavenly Principle are all established on the denaturalization of Nature or on the emptying out of Heavenly Principle from Heavenly Principle, i.e., the refusal to acknowledge that actual existence in itself is Heavenly Principle and Nature; these three views of Nature/Heavenly Principle all attempt to establish by various means a state of Nature that is differentiated from this type of actual existence. It is worth noting that one of the main characteristics of the worldview of Universal Principle is to use science and its empiricist methodology to expose the fictional essence of such naturalist categories as Heaven, the Way of Heaven, the Mandate of Heaven, and Heavenly Principle and to place Nature into objective reality, thus changing the ontological (and originary) significance of the word "Nature" *(ziran)*. The modern worldview of Universal Principle views Nature as an object that can be known and controlled, and argues that the process of the control of Nature in itself is a demonstration of the freedom of the subject. The extraction of the subject from Nature is predicated on the treatment of Nature as an objective entity that can be controlled, but the process of the control of Nature can never avoid the question of the control of society—i.e., the subject who also controls Nature. In this sense, if one wishes to think through and critique this process of modernization itself, then one must undertake a deuniversalization and denaturalization of the worldview of Universal Principle and its concept of Nature. For example, in modern history, "evolution" was seen as a kind of Universal Principle: it was seen not only as an objective narrative of history but also as a moral imperative. From the ethics of the state to social ethics, from race to gender, from the family to marriage, all varieties of changes that took place in modern society were drawn into this model of evolution. Market-oriented society was understood as a product of evolution and therefore as a kind of "natural" system, or one that accorded with Universal Principle. In this view, the modern world naturalizes another, new set of categories in order to demonstrate the legitimacy of modern society.

Across the centuries, debates about "principle" have repeatedly broken out, with each debate always leading to a denaturalization of "principle." Is "principle" the reality of the universe or the origin of the universe, or an order that is internal to our spirits? Is "principle" the relationship of rites/music formed across history, or moral rules of conduct, or a product of natural processes? Interpretations of "principle" always direct people anew toward their understanding of the actual world: Is this a world of things (wu), or a world of the heart-mind (xin)? Is this a world of institutions, or a world of Nature? Can people only understand "principle" through an understanding of the material world, or can they experience the immanence of "principle" only through the practice of daily life? Should people act according to the standards of institutions and rituals in order to fulfill "principle," or must they free themselves from all external standards and reestablish "principle" by returning anew to their own essence? Investigations of "principle" are closely linked to how people understand "things," whereas an understanding of "things" is also the only route to grasping "principle." Seeking the sources of "principle" (li) and "things" (wu) is a pursuit of the sources of critique and liberation, and an analysis of the underpinnings of order and control. By narrating the historical changes of "principle" through the ever-changing relations of "things," this method in itself already contains the historicization or deconstruction of universalist concepts of "principle" (Heavenly Principle and Universal Principle). My primary goal and method is to focus on the relationships between "principle" and "things," to investigate various aspects of "the order of things": first, changes in methods of moral judgment and historical circumstances of these changes; second, changes in methods of moral judgment and their relationship to ways that institutions of knowledge and methods of inquiry were restructured; third, the relationship between the restructuring of genealogies of knowledge and changes to social institutions. All of these questions are closely related to the question of China's modern identity: questions of identity cannot avoid leading to questions of worldviews, knowledge, and their institutions. Nationalism, modernity, and other questions are phenomena that are produced amid massive changes in institutions and knowledge, and thus a historical understanding of these questions cannot avoid taking into account the epic changes that occurred in the nineteenth century in worldviews, institutions of knowledge, institutional conditions, and material culture. If one of the main duties of modern Chinese revolutions was to transform traditional China into a nation-state, then the dissolution of the worldview of Heavenly Principle and the formation of the dominant position of the worldview of Universal Principle also conformed to this process of transformation.

FOUR

China's Modern Identity and the Transformation of Empire

1. TWO MODES OF INTERPRETING NATIONAL IDENTITY

Within the methodological framework of nineteenth-century cultural-ism, the continuity between modern China and the "Chinese empire" has generally been accepted. This narrative of continuity has produced two types of deterministic points of view that are opposed in their politi-cal orientations but actually quite similar in their historical outlook. The first type of determinism is manifested in all nationalist narratives writ-ten in the basic framework of "(Chinese) national history" *(guoshi)* from modern times onward. These histories, in turn, can be broken down into two different groups. One group begins with the myth of a common Chi-nese ancestry, using a genealogy of Confucian orthodoxy *(daotong)* ex-emplified by Emperor Yao, Emperor Shun, Yu the Great, Tang of Shang, King Wen of Zhou, King Wu of Zhou, the Duke of Zhou, Confucius, and subsequent dynasties to construct a narrative of China's historical conti-nuity. The other operates through a framework of temporal narrative cat-egories of ancient *(gudai)*, modern *(xiandai)*, and early modern *(jindai)*, supplemented by discussion of the evolution of modes of production and the development of class relations, to construct a linear, evolutionary, devel-opmental narrative of China. Both of these historical myths are expressed variously in modern slogans about "descendants of the Yellow Emperor and Flame Emperor" *(Yan Huang zisun)* and "descendants of the dragon" *(longde chuanren)* found in the mass media and textbooks, the modern ideology of making tributes to ancestors (such as the Yellow Emperor and Confucius) under the guidance of the state, and archaeological-historical projects. The second type of determinism is found in cultural-ist narratives that deconstruct the myth of a shared Chinese ancestry and of dynastic continuity. On the surface, this culturalism stands in direct opposition to the previous narrative: it demonstrates the fictional nature of the narrative of the Three Dynasties of Antiquity, points to the fact that most dynasties in China were established by peoples from outside China proper, and proves that arguments for a genealogy of continuity based on dynastic cycles simply do not obtain.[1] Yet while it explains the relationship between modern China and the "Chinese empire," this narrative also appeals to the same logic of continuity to which the previous narrative also appealed, arguing that the crisis of modern China is completely the product of unbroken cyclical history. One historian has gone so far as to argue that China's dynastic histories, with their focus on biographies and chronological history, lack a consciousness of historical time. So too, he argues, does the Chinese script; its use as a medium to produce Chinese literature, theater, music, stories, and popular culture must necessarily reproduce this "timeless" sense of time, and thus China's "past" can constantly be reborn as "the present."[2] If we say that Chinese nationalist narratives give themselves legitimacy through the historical myth of continuity, then it is also true that, even though the culturalist methodology rejects the continuity of China in terms of population, geography, and the legitimacy of its political structure, it nonetheless accepts a kind of cultural continuity that transcends national identity and dynastic change, using this continuity as evidence that China is "an empire in the guise of a modernizing unitary state."[3] This culturalism contains two important historical judgments. First, China has not made the natural transition from empire to nation-state. And, second, China is a society that lacks national unity and is held together only by an imperial tradition represented by the cultural identity of Confucianism and the imperial language of Chinese.

In the last two or three decades, scholarly reflection on and critique of nationalism has brought narratives based on the "imagined" nature and "constructedness" of the nation to the forefront. These two concepts clearly emphasize that the nation *(minzu)* is an innovation of modernity, and thus are helpful in breaking down those nationalist and culturalist historical narratives that are established on notions of historical continuity. In his widely influential work, *Imagined Communities,* Benedict Anderson defined the nation as a kind of "imagined political community," a community that was imagined to exist within certain limits and to possess sovereignty—the so-called limited and sovereign community was set in opposition to the unlimited empire and its power structure. As a modern global phenomenon, the emergence of this "imagined community" depended on the following factors: first, the gradual decline of the major elements of social unity in preindustrial society, as seen in the decline of classical monarchy, the unification of religious faith and geographical relations, and changes in views of time toward a sense of simultaneity; and, second, the large-scale expansion of print capitalism (especially newspapers, literature, and textbooks), which created the possibility for the formation of new national vernaculars and for the organization of different groups of people into the same space of "homogenous, empty time" described in Walter Benjamin's "Theses on the Philosophy of History" (1940). According to Anderson, nationalism spread from North America and Europe to other places around the world, resulting in one wave after another of official nationalism or popular nationalism. The political model provided by the previous wave was always reproduced by the wave that followed it, ultimately paving the way for a world system of nation-states.[4] The widespread rise in literacy rates and expansions of commerce, industry, mass media, and organs of the state were all important features of nineteenth-century Europe, as each monarchy saw within its borders the emergence of powerful forces that drove the pursuit of a unified vernacular language.[5] Faced with this vernacular nationalism, even if Latin was the official state language, it could not serve as the language of commerce, the language of science, the language of print, or the language of literature. Whether in the mass nationalism of nineteenth-century Europe or in the vernacular nationalism of Southeast Asia, "language" (as a tool of the imagination) and print culture became essential media for imagining the nation.

2. CHINESE IDENTITY AND PROBLEMS OF LANGUAGE

Just as the "imagined community" is not an "imaginary" or "fictional community," the concept of "imagined" absolutely cannot be equated with "false consciousness" or fantasy. It merely denotes that the formation of communities is closely related to people's identities, aspirations, desires, imagined relationships, and the material conditions that underwrite these identities and imaginings. Feelings of historical continuity and community are all products of imagining, but they are not merely fictional stories, for they contain the conditions by which this imagining may be produced. They are found, for example, in the continuity between modes of daily life that persist through the change from one dynasty to another; in the historical outlook and views on ritual provided by Confucianism that make it possible for "foreign dynasties" to become Chinese dynasties; in the unique, ever-changing views of space and time embedded in daily life and Confucian thought; and in the political forms produced by the expansion of capitalism. The decline of monarchical rule and the development of print capitalism, as well as the temporal-historical views centered on the nation that were produced as a result of these two processes, all played similarly important historical roles in China from the late Qing onward. However, rather than argue that these factors were forces by which modern Chinese identity was produced, it is better to say that they served as conditions for the modern renewal of Chinese identity. If modern China is the product of imperial self-transformation, then a national identity that serves as a consciousness of political community certainly must be rooted within the imperial tradition, and therefore is not a purely modern phenomenon. In this sense, print capitalism cannot be seen as an indispensable precondition of this "imagined community" in China. On this point, the question of dialects and vernaculars can serve to illustrate the question. The formation of a modern nation-state clearly has a close historical relationship to the creation of a written language based on the vernacular. Jacob Burkhardt's *The Civilization of the Renaissance in Italy* has described how Dante Alighieri's vernacular compositions stood in opposition to Latin and established the dialect of Tuscany as the foundation of a new national language[6]; that popular literature and print culture provided a medium for and the force behind vernacular nationalism. In East Asia, both Japan and Korea used their own vernaculars to resist the influence of Chinese, creating their own national written languages. It is for these reasons that Karatani Kōjin has argued that phonocentrism—or, more accurately, vernacular nationalism—is not merely a "Western" question because in the process of nation-state formation, "the same problem has emerged all over the world without exception."[7] The "ancient learning" *(kogaku)* movement of eighteenth-century Japan is one case in point. However, from the late Qing onward, print culture and the revolution in language were not directed toward vernacular nationalism, but were centered on the imperial written language, working to unify various dialects and bring the local onto conduits connected with the "national." This phenomenon, unique to language-reform movements in China, was closely related to the conditions within the empire that made possible the emergence of all state-building movements in modern China.

Even if we examine these questions from the perspective of the relationship between phonocentrism and nationalism, these particular historical conditions must still be given equal importance. The vernacular language movement in Chinese society emerged from the "church Romanization movement" launched by European missionaries during the Ming and Qing periods. This movement sought to use the Roman alphabet to transcribe the dialects of various regions and translate and transmit the Bible and Christian reading materials. This movement was interested neither in forming regional identities nor in national forms, but in bringing the writing of the vernacular and the teachings of Catholicism together, thus resulting in internal linkages between the vernacular movement and religious identity. In the late-Qing period, the work of this "church Romanization movement" gradually transformed into the "National Language Romanization *(Guoyu luomazi)* movement," an effort promoted by the gentry to use the Roman alphabet to write Mandarin Chinese and to undertake surveys of pronunciation from various regions that would serve as a basis for a shared national pronunciation. This movement was inspired by vernacular language movements that took place in Japan and elsewhere, but did not follow the same route as European countries or that of Japan's vernacular nationalism. First, the National Language Romanization movement was not interested in breaking away from a standard, universal language—written Mandarin Chinese—but rather sought to create a system of pronunciation that, drawing from the various regional languages, was also suited to a universal written Mandarin Chinese. For this reason, we can see this movement as the precursor to the founding of the Society for Unified Pronunciation *(Guoyin tongyi hui)* in 1913. Second, movements focusing on language are perhaps less the unique product of nationalism than they are the results of developments that emerged from planned language change during the imperial era. In the eighth year of the Yongzheng reign (1730), the inability of people from Fujian and Guangdong to speak *guanhua* ("official speech") led the imperial court to order the establishment of Academies for Correct Pronunciation *(Zhengyin guan)* in four cities in these provinces and to decree that lower-level examination candidates who could not speak correct *guanhua* would not be able to take the examinations for three years. In 1733, the rule was extended for another three years. From these cultural policies put in place during the imperial era, we see that the rulers' efforts to regulate the customs among the people in fact emphasized the written language because the standard for correct pronunciation was *guanhua* pronunciation. In this case, however, *guanhua* pronunciation was not the spoken dialect of the Beijing region, but the language internally regulated by the written language of officialdom. Common, or "vulgar," words and phrases *(su zi su yu)* that would be found in any vernacular are not to be found in the "proper pronunciation" of this standard language. In his discussion of this issue, Kang Youwei wrote:

> We should circulate guides for writing throughout the realm, so that every book on heaven and earth, ghosts and spirits, human conduct, royal affairs, and things and events all use the ancient to illuminate the present and are written in an elegant style; even the use of grammatical particles *(zhuci)* can be regulated and their usages promulgated everywhere. . . . Taking these regulations as [official] language, they can be spread from the central provinces to the border territories, so that all must use it. When writing has been regu-

larized, then all types of writing can follow established forms, including public and private correspondence, biographies and records, and prefaces and essays. Prefectures and districts (*fu* and *xian*) would not be referred to "sectors" and "fiefs" (*du* and *yi*) . . . Shanxi and Shaanxi would not be called *Qin* and *Jin;* all names would appear according to contemporary usage, with no use of archaism. This [policy] would allow greater ease in reading for all people, from the educated to the unlettered, and thus the people's knowledge would increase daily, and knowledge and learning would be broadened. Both forms of writing and their style should be regulated, so that no one can single-handedly take up another way of writing.[8]

From this comment it is evident that some connections did indeed exist between late-Qing phonocentrism and nationalism and the creation of a new national language, but this connection continued to work along the lines of an imperial language, not in terms of the structure of vernacular nationalism.

When the language reform movement based on speech and pronunciation gave way to a language reform movement based on written language, this trend became even clearer. Up until the 1930s, the revolution in language sparked by the May Fourth Movement was a key part of the movement for a modern national culture, but its main emphasis was not to be found in the relationship between vernacular nationalism and the imperial language, but in the oppositional relationships, expressed in terms of class and culture, between the aristocracy and the common people, or between the elites and the masses and between tradition and science. The core problem of the language movement shifted from the question of pronunciation to the problem of a universal language—that is, a written language. During the New Culture movement and efforts to promote national educational policies and modern urban commerce, literary and scientific publications and educational materials for elementary and middle schools gradually cast off the influence of classical Chinese, substituting it with a vernacular written language (*baihuawen*) that could be used in commerce and science as well as in newspapers and other popular reading materials. The movement for *baihuawen* (written vernacular), however, cannot in any way be seen as a vernacular movement. More-over, as a system for written language, the substitution of classical Chi-nese by *baihuawen* cannot be described as phonocentrism. It is not a question of a national language taking the place of an imperial language, as was the case when Italian, French, and English took the place of Latin, or when the Tokyo dialect or the Seoul dialect were used to create a new national language. The question in this case is one of one type of Chinese system of writing taking the place of another type of Chinese system of writing. This period also saw the emergence of a movement (which was not implemented) to abandon the Chinese character script, as well as a largely ineffective movement to adopt Esperanto. Neither movement, however, pushed for a national vernacular; instead, they sought to bring an internationalist orientation into efforts to reform the Chinese written language. In this sense, all of the language reform movements just de-scribed showed themselves to be far more interested in "modern iden-tity" or the modern form of national identity as such rather than a partic-ular national identity.

The largest-scale vernacular language movement of the twentieth century occurred during the War of Resistance against Japan (1937–1945). With the occupation of major cities, the center of the national culture shifted from urban areas to the vast countryside, giving rise to a cultural movement that worked not through print culture but through the forms of oral literature. The transfer of political, cultural, and economic centers from developed cities to the distant interior was a time of exceptional reversal in the direction of social mobility in modern Chinese society. This vernacular language movement was closely related to the war of re-sistance, military mobilization, and social mobilization. The culture and politics of this era needed to reach the widest possible groups of com-pletely illiterate peasants and soldiers, and thus it was not the written language and print culture, represented by newspapers and literary peri-odicals, but local patois and local cultural forms that became key materials for social exchange and social mobilization. It was not literary and artistic forms such as fiction, essays, modern poems, and modern plays that served as the major media for literature and art, but drum ballads (*guci*), songs, storytelling, rhyming dialogues (*duikouci*), street plays, and local opera.

As everyday speech, dialect, and local culture rose in status, a new kind of print culture completely different from the Mandarin written language emerged, one that used the Latin alphabet to produce in great numbers printed materials—magazines, textbooks, and other items—written in dialects. The Latinization movement originated from language practices among Red Army soldiers and workers in the far eastern regions of the Soviet Union and was later introduced into China by Qu Qiubai (1899–1935) and others, finding a much broader audience during the War of Resistance against Japan. In formal terms, this language-reform movement most closely resembles the vernacular nationalisms found in Europe and in other regions because it involved vernacular pronunciation and written forms and completely changed the status of the universal imperial written language. From the beginning, however, the vernacular movement and Latinization movement were absorbed into the logic of "national characteristics" *(minzu xing):* the mass national movement did not develop in the direction of vernacular nationalism, but rather yoked the question of the vernacular and local cultures together with the questions of national characteristics or "the all-national" *(quanguoxing).* Within this movement, then, we ultimately do not in fact see a political orientation toward vernacular nationalism. With the conclusion of the War of Resistance against Japan, this vernacular cultural movement drew to a close.[9] Therefore, because it is neither vernacular nor local, and yet is a kind of identity that can contain the vernacular and local culture and politics, the precondition for China to become an "imagined community" is the national consciousness rooted in rural Chinese peasant society *(nongcun shehui)* that was created through the large-scale social dislocation caused by war. Far from being completely modern creations, this "imagined community" and its identity are the products of a nation forming over a long period of history through continuously changing derivations of language, institutions, faiths, myths, and ways of living.[10] It is a mode and force through which national struggles and the modern party politics of national movements bind local culture to the demands of nationalism.[11] Like the vernacular nationalisms of Europe, nationalist movements in Japan, Korea, and Vietnam all sought to resist and break free from the imperial Chinese language. By comparison, the relationship between

China's vernacular language movement and Chinese national identity is a unique phenomenon. The vernacular language movement did not result in a nationalist movement that threatened Chinese identity. In this case, national identity is not a single process that brings all groups and individuals into a unified identity. Moreover, the formation of modern national languages has never taken as an explicit goal the elimination of dialects or minority languages. Just as the revival of local culture and the promotion of dialects during the War of Resistance against Japan did not constitute an obstacle to national identity, national identity itself also cannot eliminate local, dialect culture or community, local, or religious identity or identification.

In this sense, any method that attempts to get away from the essential political-historical issues and discuss nationalism and national identity only in terms of the vernacular, print culture, and written language will be badly hobbled. In cultural movements from the late Qing onward, what was truly new was not to be found in the national subject *(minzu zhuti)*, but in the political form of the sovereign state; in the inherent relationship between the leap in development in commerce and industrial capital on the one hand and the nation-state on the other; in the organic interaction between the revolutionary force of scientific technology and its worldview and nationalism; in the relationship between a genealogy of knowledge that sprang from modern, urban education and a new national identity; in a mode of identification that extracted the individual from the extended family, the local, and other mechanisms of collective identification and organized him or her directly into an identification with the nation-state, as well as the new concepts of responsibilities and rights that were produced by this process—it was under these conditions that the national subject was made new. All of these issues must be understood as part of the transformational relationship between China's imperial tradition and modern national culture, as part of the international nature of social change. Within the internationalist tendencies of the May Fourth Movement, national identity and internationalism could even constitute a mutually supportive relationship. In this sense, modern identity need not be equated with a purely national identity (especially not ethnic identity), including local, international, and other multiple models of identity and identification. In times of war and crisis, these models of identification were absorbed into systems of national identity and often were subsumed into the dominant discourses of the nation-state. Chinese identity, however, never denied the significance of multiple identifications or the changing nature of dialect culture. (The decline of dialect culture and minority languages is more closely related to contemporary processes of the expansion of the market economy.) With respect to questions of national identity, the central problems of the local, the international, and cultural hybridity drew attention from all quarters in cultural debates and historical scholarship in the nineteenth and twentieth centuries. Contemporary scholarship on nationalism emphasizes the ways that national identity absorbs and suppresses local identity, but if such discussions abandon a detailed examination of the social forces behind this absorption and suppression—especially modern capitalism—and see this suppressing mechanism as the result of imperial tradition, then they cannot explain why Qing-dynasty imperial culture was able to contain Manchu, Mongolian, Han, Hui, Tibetan, and other official languages and diverse political-legal systems, as well as extremely rich and diverse local cultures. This brief discussion should suffice to show that seeing the "imagined community" as a purely modern phenomenon offers no way to explain the transformation that China has undergone.

One classic feature of nationalism is that it uses language to define national characteristics. Culturalists explain China's unity in terms of the unifying qualities of the Chinese language, whereas postmodernist nationalist narratives also explain modern Chinese national identity in terms of print culture and language movements. These two completely different methodologies are both influenced by the way nationalism defines the nation. In this framework of knowledge, the current unity of China is explained in terms of the lack of a vernacular nationalism (or the stability of the Chinese written language's unifying properties), and thus China's political crisis is also explained as the result of the absence of political nationalism and of the continuity of imperial culture. Even nineteenth-century European nationalist linguists, however, did not argue for a simple predestined relationship between language and the nation. Karl Wilhelm von Humboldt (1767–1835), a representative figure among nineteenth-century German comparative linguists, attempted to show that language had a structural influence on the human spirit, but he also admitted that the actions produced by the forms and laws of language are passive and limited, whereas the actions that humans perform on language are active and unlimited: "It [language] cannot, under any circumstances, become an absolute *restraint* upon man."[12] The discovery of oracle bones from the Yin and Shang dynasties has demonstrated the unusual staying power of Chinese characters. The Chinese written language undoubtedly spurred on the absorption and assimilation of the various peoples and regions that are now contained within the map of today's China. This history provides evidence that different groups of people are able to coexist and share a common cultural experience. Even so, the unity of the Chinese language and the unity of a political framework could not arise at the same time. The imperial dynasties of China's past were not merely dynasties based on language, nor were they empires based on a single nationality, and, even more so, they were not necessarily empires based on the rule of Han people. The permeation in the Middle Ages of northern peoples such as the Xianbei and Tuoba into China proper, along with the massive empire established by the Mongols and Jurchens, are extremely important historical antecedents for a large part of what now makes up China's geography, culture, and population. China's populations, nationalities, and geography are products of innumerable interminglings, migrations, wars, and exchanges. In an unending series of changes of surnames, changes in clothing and costume, and interethnic marriages, it is already impossible for us to point conclusively a single Han nationality or to use "scientific means" to separate out individual bloodlines from the so-called Han nationality. From ancient times to the present, languages from completely different language families and an endlessly rich array of dialects (linguists separate Chinese into seven major dialects: Northern, Wu, Hunan, Gan [Jiangxinese], Hakka, Min [Fujianese], and Yue [Cantonese], each with a vast number of subdialects) formed a unique aspect of what we call Chinese culture.[13] Every period of historical change and intermixing of populations also brought major changes in language. These changes, in turn, served as the basis for the methods used by Qing-dynasty "evidential learning" *(kaozheng)* scholars to investigate ancient pronunciations of Chinese characters (especially historical phonology).

The unity of the Chinese language cannot be considered to be directly related to the question of the political unity of empire: the Manchus, Mongols, Tibetans, and Muslim populations all had their own written languages, but during the Mongol and Manchu dynasties, this did not result in a fragmented nation-state or empire. By the same token, Korea, Japan, and Vietnam all used the Chinese written language for long stretches of history, but these countries did not became part of China as a result of their shared written language. Moreover, each of these countries created a new national identity through their own respective vernacular nationalisms. Why is it that dynastic states that were so close in terms of writing and culture and that saw such close collaboration between groups during the process of revolution did not, through the process of revolution or reform, transform into a unified state? In regard to this question, there are at least two factors at play. First, even in the succession of dynasties before the nineteenth century, dynastic states that were so closely related to Chinese culture and Chinese dynasties maintained their own sense of identity and independent political structures, and, within the framework of the tribute system, remained autonomous political entities. In this sense, shared cultural essence is not the only condition for the formation of a unified nation-state, just as cultural difference also need not serve as a historical precondition for the separation of different political entities. Arguments, then, that China has only a cultural identity and not a political identity are grossly oversimplified. Second, the formation of the nineteenth-century nation-state hinged upon the division of the spheres of territorial power established by colonial states, which differed vastly from the political-economic relations that existed in the dynastic era. In the early years of the Chinese revolution, any alliance that encroached upon the interests of England, France, Japan, Russia, or other imperial powers was impossible. In 1907, when Zhang Taiyan first put forward his idea of the "Republic of China," he adopted the model of the European nation-state, attempting to found a China on the basis of a single (Han) ethnicity and culture. In his widely influential essay entitled "The Meaning of the 'Republic of China'" (*Zhonghua Minguo jie*), he used the traditional Chinese concepts of "outer territories and domains" (*dian* and *fu*) to present the following analysis: countries such as Korea, Vietnam, and Burma historically and culturally had close cultural ties to China, but if these countries were to form a single allied state with China, this would certainly touch off military intervention by major powers such as Japan, France, and England in the newly formed Republic of China. On the contrary, however, the ethnic groups, cultures, and religions of northwestern China may be quite different from that of southeastern China, but for historical and geographical reasons, including these regions in the new Republic would not result in direct intervention by European colonial powers. For this reason, then, this most radical of late Qing nationalists did not imagine his "Republic of China" strictly along the lines of such factors as ethnicity, language, and religion.[14] The colonial world order and its threat of intervention were the most important forces that shaped movements in the early twentieth century to establish a Chinese nation and the scope of its territorial sovereignty.

3. CONFUCIANISM AND CHINESE IDENTITY IN MINORITY-RULE DYNASTIES

Political systems are living things, always adapting to social and economic changes, avoiding contradictions that arise from failure to adapt. The French historian Jacques Gernet (1921–) once very wisely said that it is a methodological error to offer an overall definition of China as an imperial society or as an empire. For example, whether in terms of culture or in terms of overall institutions, major differences can be found between the Song and the Ming eras, with their systems of centralized administration and imperial power, and the Qing dynasty, with its system of imperial power, which synthesized the Khanate system of rule and imperial rule. Under the surface of the idea of China's unified imperial system, there have always been changes wrought by differences within and between state organizations, social groups, regions, ethnic groups, and religious faiths. Without this type of nuanced historical understanding, we have no way to explain the endlessly changing, always newly created historical meaning of "China." It is from this perspective that categories of historical relationships that once had been subsumed under the rubrics of China's institutions (land distribution and management, bureaucratic systems, the military, the examination system, imperial power, etc.), culture (language, customs, Confucian learning, Buddhism, popular religion, etc.), and ethnicity (new social relations produced by the collision, combination, and transformation of languages, cultures, and institutions) cannot be laid out according to a lineage of Emperor Yao, Emperor Shun, Yu the Great, Tang of Shang, King Wen of Zhou, King Wu of Zhou, the Duke of Zhou, Confucius, and Confucianism; they also cannot be placed on a Han-centric political timeline of dynastic succession. The so-called pure Han nationality and the image of its imperial culture has always been a fantasy for this reason, too. In discussing the meaning of the concept of "China," we must ask the following questions: Once the Xianbei, Tuoba, Muslims, Jewish people, and other groups took power or migrated to China proper, how were they gradually fused into a larger social community? And when forced to live among others, how did they maintain their own identity? Once these groups had defeated and conquered the dynasties of China proper, why did northern peoples—including Mongolians and Manchus—transform themselves into Chinese dynasties, establishing a multipolar framework of power within a set period of time and scope? The concept of dynastic cycles contains the problem of the legitimacy of rule: How do so-called foreign dynasties transform themselves into Chinese dynasties, and why are these dynasties able to be recognized within the tribute system and system of international relations as the legitimate representatives of Chinese dynasties? If we do not answer these questions, then we also have no way to understand the meaning of "China" amid all other historical changes, and it also becomes very difficult to understand why critiques of linear views of history and Han-centric versions of China do not result in a deconstruction of the idea of "China." If they are to produce meaningful results, discussions in Chinese studies about "sinicization" and "foreignization" *(Huhua)* need to address specific historical relationships and not get caught up in political correctness.

Language, ethics, and customs certainly play a role in political unity and its symbolism, but unity and its symbolism also need a special political

culture and a special theory of dynastic legitimacy to serve as a fundamental historical precedent and political grounding. Thus the theory of
Confucian "orthodoxy" *(zhengtong)* or ritualism that gradually formed
from the Han dynasty onward, along with the model of dynastic cycles
that took shape based on this orthodoxy, plays an extremely important
role. This model created the continuity of "China" amid continuously
changing geographical and ethnic relations. In other words, according to
this model, what constitutes a crucial difference between China and
other multinational empires can be described as follows: unification of the
Chinese empire not only relies on a lateral dynamics of power between
center and margin, but also relies on a longitudinal relation of temporal-
historical succession, i.e., a dynastic cycle established on the theory of
Confucian moral orthodoxy. The establishment of a linear genealogy of
Chinese history is closely related to this theory of moral orthodoxy and
ritualism because it is precisely according to this theory of "orthodoxy"
that those dynasties made up of ethnic minorities that defeated Han rulers and took control of China proper could insert themselves into the
model of cyclical dynastic rule. The revival during the Qing dynasty of
research on the Gongyang commentary to the *Spring and Autumn Annals* demonstrated that Gongyang learning did not disappear with the
decline of New Text learning in the Eastern Han dynasty. On the contrary, this Confucian theory of moral orthodoxy (especially its theory of
"grand unification" [*yitong*] and "linking the three systems" [*tong san
tong*]) had already become a theoretical resource and ritual basis by which
later dynasties would establish themselves as legitimate. The Jin dynasty,
long the nemesis of the Song dynasty, used Confucian orthodoxy—
especially large-scale unified governance *(da yi tong)*—to assert the orthodoxy of its rule. The Mongol empire that followed the Jin—and that
wiped out the Song—also used Confucian arguments about orthodoxy
(especially from the *Spring and Autumn Annals*) to show that it had taken
up the orthodox and legitimate position of previous Chinese dynasties.[15]
Gentry elites in this period also saw the Gongyang tradition of the *Spring
and Autumn Annals* as the basis for legal tradition. The founders of the
Qing dynasty brought together the Mongol khan system and the imperial
rulership of the Ming dynasty under the banner of "linking three sys-

tems" *(tong san tong),* and used the orthodox position of Confucianism to insert themselves into the genealogy of Chinese dynasties. For this reason, the theory of Confucian moral orthodoxy and its rituals was exactly what provided outside minority groups with a basis for establishing a "Chinese dynasty" that could transcend national characteristics and even language and cultural differences. In this sense, "Chinese" identity is not produced through Han-centric narratives, but through the ways in which different nationalities claim legitimacy for themselves as they establish new dynastic eras—that is, the ways in which they remake or transform themselves into Chinese dynasties. For this reason, then, Confucian orthodoxy cannot be equated with Confucian doctrine from the pre-Qin period and cannot be seen merely as a kind of Han-centric view of history. The continuous development of orthodoxy is closely related to the ways that different dynasties—including minority-rule dynasties—seek political legitimacy for themselves. At the same time, the development of orthodoxy is also tied together in constantly changing historical relationships with the remaking and redefinition of ethical values, institutional forms, and modes of living.[16]

It is precisely in this sense, then, that we have to return to simple dismissals of the way Confucianism distinguishes between foreigners and Chinese *(Yi Xia zhi bian)* and ask some of the following questions: What kind of latent capacities were contained within Confucianism that allowed for those who made use of it to overcome racial and cultural differences and provide legitimacy for foreign dynasties? In culture since the late Qing and in historical writing since that time, the "distinction between foreign and Chinese" *(Yi Xia zhi bian)* has long been portrayed as a key reason why the Chinese empire and its humanistic tradition had been cut off from the outside world. Karl Marx saw the Great Wall as both a sign of China's suspicion of foreign barbarians and its self-isolation, arguing that only the onslaught of cheap capitalist goods could bring the wall crashing down.[17] But was the Great Wall really the product of the distinction between foreign and Chinese, as people imagined it to be? As far back as the 1940s, Owen Lattimore described a lively Inner Asian region centered on the Great Wall. The focus on the Great Wall in this account of China and Inner Asia not only went beyond common historical narratives that focused on agriculture around the Yellow River or cities, trade, and agriculture around the Grand Canal or the Jiangnan region, but also went beyond the historical outlook that was based on the framework of political institutions and state borders. The "Great Wall as center" refers to social entities that existed on both sides of the Great Wall: agricultural society and nomadic society. These two societies undertook long-term interactions with one another around the Great Wall, and thus both societies left a deep imprint on one another. Nomadic peoples were not naturally nomadic; they were a part of society that was in fact cast out during the development of agricultural society and took up residence in the grassland regions. To adjust to the natural environment of the grassland regions, they gradually gave up agriculture, transforming into nomadic peoples. It was only when this type of division of labor developed to a certain stage that this society would transform itself from one on the margins of agricultural society to a grassland society. For this reason, agricultural society and nomadic society developed alongside one another, interacting organically. The history of the interactions between the two led to what is called "the frontier style."[18] Over a long period of time, then, the Great Wall served as a belt of connections and interactions. Jacques Gernet pointed out three major forms of connections and interactions: commercial flows (maritime trade and overland caravans), military expansion and diplomatic relations, and religious proselytizing and pilgrimages.[19] With the unification of territory brought about by the Qing dynasty, the Great Wall no longer served as a symbol demarcating the inside and outside the territorial boundaries, but rather became the hinterland of the Qing empire. This new reality was reflected by the Kangxi emperor's decision in 1681 to issue an edict forbidding any new work to repair the Great Wall.

This is not to say, however, that within the empire regulations related to prohibition and isolation created by ethnic rule had been done away with, or that the hierarchies established on the set of regulations related to prohibition and isolation had disappeared. For the originary territories of the Manchus and the Mongolians, the Qing dynasty issued a number of regulations limiting people from southeastern China from entering those places and strictly forbidding Han Chinese from entering into marriage with Manchus and Mongolians. Using a new means of distinguishing between "inner" (the Manchu Eight Banners) and "outer" (Han Chinese), the Qing court not only implemented a series of prohibition policies but also used laws and edicts to cement differences between ethnic groups. The true movement to break through the separation between inner and outer was less the unification of the empire than the reverse immigration flows caused by the empire's subjugation of China proper, as well as the continuous intermingling that occurred during daily life: virtually the same time that the Qing forces entered China and large numbers of people from outside of the borders flowed into the central regions, a substantial number of people living in southeastern China migrated legally and illegally to these outer areas, renting land, conducting trade, marrying local people, and creating a situation of "intermingling" of Manchu bannergroups and commoners. The Great Wall once again became a belt that drew together agricultural society and nomadic society. All of the social migrations that broke through the official isolation policies served as challenges to the absolute yardstick that would distinguish between inner and outer, foreign and Chinese, and acted to shape new relationships of identity. As a kind of specific yet constantly changing historical relationship, the meaning of "China" cannot be separated from these kinds of practices—including the way peoples of different ethnicities and regions broke through fences of political isolation, interacted with one another, and practiced coexistence. The suppression of cultural diversity in official histories is also the suppression of this type of interaction and coexistence in popular history.

The distinction between Chinese and foreign and inner and outer were important issues for scholarship of Confucius's time and also involved issues related to Confucian ritual. As happens with many concepts, behind the continuity of the categories of "Chinese" and "foreign" and "inner" and "outer" lay completely different historical forces and meanings. Following the Opium Wars, Wei Yuan (1794–1856) suggested "learning superior foreign techniques to defend against the barbarians," providing the Foreign Affairs Movement (*yangwu yundong*) with an important theoretical basis. This motto, however, also contained the historical traces of debates about the distinctions between Chinese and foreigners. The form of sovereignty of the nation-state and nationalist theory contained distinctions between races, geographical boundaries, and distinctions between inner and outer in terms of sovereign relations: Are these not also a set of ideas about closing off from the outside world? Debates about Chinese/foreign issues in late Qing conceal a basic fact: in over two hundred years of Qing rule, "the distinctions between Chinese and foreign" in Confucian learning did not occupy a mainstream position. Debates about "the distinctions between Chinese and foreign" during the late Qing are less a manifestation of Confucian tradition than a response to foreign aggression and European nationalism. For a long period of time, the Qing dynasty had been seen by Han people as a foreign political power, and its legitimacy could not be established on the basis of the Confucian tradition of supporting "barriers between Chinese and foreigners" (*Yi Xia zhi fang*). From the seventeenth century onward, the Qing dynasty established an autocratic political system based on minority ethnic rule while it used the motto of "Manchu-Han unity" to critique the concept of "barriers between Chinese and foreigners." It also calmed tensions between Manchus and Han through ritual sacrifices to Confucius, the reinstatement of the imperial examination system, its support of the patriarchal clan system, adoption of the Ming legal code, and the employment of Han officials. For a dynasty to establish its own legitimacy, a major aspect of its imperial ideology needed to eliminate the absolute differences between Chinese and foreign, inner and outer. In the late Ming and early Qing, essays such as "Casting off Barbarians" (*Rang Yi lun*) by Wang Fuzhi (1619–1692) and "Distinctions between Barbarians and Chinese" (*Yi Xia zhi bian*) by Lü Liuliang (1629–1683) were popular for a time among Ming loyalists, but were always on the receiving end of Qing official suppression. The *Records of Great Righteousness Resolving Confusion* (*Dayi juemi lu*), composed by the Yongzheng emperor to refute the work of Lü Liuliang's disciple Zeng Jing (1679–1736), also vigorously attacked the "distinction between Chinese and barbarians."

If we say that official Qing discourses on "unity between Manchu and Han" were intended to reduce resistance from Han people and that they also served to transform the Manchu Qing dynasty effectively into a multinational "Chinese dynasty," then it follows that the discussions of "oppositions between Chinese and foreigners" that gradually became popular in the eighteenth century among Han gentry elites demonstrated a certain critique from Han elites at the bottom of the ethnic hierarchy that was directed toward policies of ethnic isolation, ethnic hierarchy, and ethnic-based institutions, even as they accepted the rule of the Qing court. On the basis of ritual, they severed the relationship between the concept of "China" and the categories of ethnicity and geography. Even if their political positions were starkly different, this distinction was the same as the one made by Gu Yanwu at the beginning of the Qing dynasty in the distinctions he made between "losing all under heaven" (*wang tianxia*) and "losing the state" (*wang guo*). In both cases, these distinctions were rooted in Confucian views of ritual and understanding of historical change produced from the Confucian worldview. In this sense, to understand prohibition and isolation policies as an effect of Confucianism is to confuse the fundamental and the incidental. For example, during the mid Qing period, New Text scholars reexamined the principles laid out in the *Luxuriant Dew of the Spring and Autumn Annals* (*Chunqiu fanlu*) that honor ritual and stress trustworthiness, value trustworthiness over place of origin, and hold the importance of ritual over that of oneself to emphasize that any standard of deciding whether or not something was "Chinese" that was based on geography or "person" (ethnic identity) was out of line with the principles of ritual. Working within the framework New Text scholarship, men such as Zhuang Cunyu (1719–1788), Liu Fenglu (1774–1829), and Wei Yuan criticized the Qing state's policies of ethnic hierarchy. References in their works to important themes from classical texts appear frequently in their work: "When Chinese become barbaric, they must be treated as barbarians" (*Zhongguo er yidi, ze yidi zhi*); "When barbarians enter China, they become Chinese" (*yidi ru Zhongguo, ze Zhongguo zhi*); and "China is now completely barbaric" (*Zhongguo yi yi xin yidi ye*). All of these statements emphasize that ritual and culture (rather than geography or ethnicity) define the importance of "China" and offer a pointed critique of the view of China promoted by Song-dynasty neo-Confucianism that called for "separation between Chinese and foreigners." The "relativization of Chinese and foreign" is found neither in the teachings of the *Spring and Autumn Annals* nor in the doctrine of the Gongyang commentary, but in the explication of the meaning of the *Spring and Autumn Annals* offered by Dong Zhongshu (179–104 B.C.E) during the Western Han in *Luxuriant Dew of the Spring and Autumn Annals*. Dong argued that, with the expansion of the Western Han dynasty, ideas about geography used during the Zhou dynasty to distinguish between inner and outer and Chinese and foreign could no longer be applied to what was now a unified empire; those who had once been considered foreigners now had to be granted the position of Chinese *(Xia)*. To eliminate ethnic differences within the dynasty and to promote relativization of inner and outer, Qing dynasty discourses also redefined the meaning of "China": if ritual became the most important standard by which to distinguish foreigners and Chinese, then that also implies the possibility for transformation—if what is foreign were to submit to ritual, then it could also become "Chinese," just as if "China" were to betray ritual, then "China" would no longer be "China."[20] This argument shows that, at least at the normative level, it is not ethnicity, geography, or political power, but rather ritual relationships that served as the most important yardstick for political identity under the Qing. This classical "republican" ideal was echoed often in Qing-dynasty politics.

Through discussion centered on ritual relationships, Qing dynasty gentry elites relativized ideas of foreign/Chinese and inner/outer to critique ethnic relations in the empire, and thereby managed to bring to the surface, in a very subtle and muted way, the question of power and equality within the empire. This relativization of foreign/Chinese also expanded the meaning of "China," providing a framework for a Chinese identity that went beyond ethnicity. Around the time of the Opium Wars, Gong Zizhen (1792–1841), Wei Yuan, and others brought this relativization of foreign/Chinese into their understanding of East-West relations, providing the preconditions for studying the West and promoting reform in a way that was internal to Confucian thought.[21] In the sense that I discussed earlier, this concept of China certainly cannot be seen as an unchanging essence, but rather is a concept that is constantly being constructed. "China" as a concept was used both by the ruling peoples as evidence of their legitimacy and by the ruled peoples as a way to appeal for equality. As a changing historical relationship, "China" has been defined by dynasties of many different nationalities, including by minority nationalities. Invasions by northern peoples into China proper and invasions by dynasties from China proper into the "barbarian" northern territories were all filled with much blood and cruelty. The use of "China" as a category to eliminate absolute differences between inner and outer and foreign and Chinese and to form an egalitarian Chinese identity premised on the acknowledgment of the uniqueness of each ethnic group and its culture provided a new ideal by which nations could be reconciled, ethnic groups could coexist, and wars be brought to an end. Certainly, this use of "China" was only an ideal, but it would truly be an act of historical nihilism to argue that this ideal was only a historical fiction (or a display of wild arrogance by the central state) and that it bore no relationship to specific historical relations, particular political cultures, and varieties of lifestyles, as well as ancient theories of political legitimacy. The modes of self-identification that emerged under dynastic unity, the interspersing of Manchu banner groups among the common people, and the relativization by Han gentry of distinctions between foreigners and Chinese all had an important influence on the diverse social patterns and institutional structures of the Qing dynasty.

The preceding is but a brief sketch of how four major areas of New Text learning addressed by Kang Youwei in the late Qing could offer an understanding of how the distinction between Chinese and foreigners became key elements of modern Chinese identity: first, he confirmed that the contemporary world was entering into an era in which many states stood in contention with one another, just as in the Spring and Autumn period, and argued that "China" should restructure its relationship between itself and the world. Kang Youwei refused to use the concept of the nation-state to define the meaning of China, arguing that "China" had become a complete and unified entity through historical change. According to this line of thought, it is change and multiplicity, not a single source and single nationality, that constitute the essential meaning of "China," and Kang's Confucian learning is a theory formed on the basis of these changes and multiplicities. Second, in the opposition with Old Text classical learning, Kang upheld Confucius as Sage-King and New King *(Xin wang)*; his refusal to grant the usual historical high recognition given to the Duke of Zhou in fact worked to cast Confucius in the role of an emperor *(wangzhe)*. Thus, on the basis of cultural identity, Kang established the emperor as an absolute center and locus of orthodoxy, rejecting any power relations resulting from regency forms of government. This position is the result of efforts to rethink the role of the emperor under the regency of Empress Cixi (1835–1908) as well as a theoretical confirmation of the unity of imperial sovereignty. Third, Kang's attempts to affirm the centrality of the power of the emperor by establishing Confucius in the position of the "New King" placed the ritual-political system of Confucianism higher than that of the emperor himself, thus laying the theoretical ground for new state political reforms. Moreover, this elevation of Confucius also restructured the representative role of the emperor: as the highest symbol of Confucian ritual, imperial power did not represent the power of a single ethnic group (i.e., Manchus) or a particular class, but represented "China." Fourth, by restructuring his cosmology through modern scientific knowledge, Kang Youwei drew Confucian universalism into a set of world relations organized according to natural principles, thus laying the groundwork for a system of natural principles related to the universe, human beings, and ethics.[22]

4. TERRITORIAL EXPANSION, INTERNATIONAL RELATIONS, AND QUESTIONS OF SOVEREIGNTY IN THE IMPERIAL AGE

As a multinational empire, the unification of the Qing dynasty was established through complex structural relationships between imperial power and feudal power (arguments about the imperial system completely killing off the old feudal aristocratic system are, at a minimum, greatly oversimplified). Looking at the larger trends, however, this type of multipolar state of affairs was not at all stable. Beginning in the seventeenth century, the process of empire building contained tensions between forces for diversity and uniformity, but the process toward the convergence of systems was nonetheless a long-term trend. The multiple centers of imperial power were expressed in two major ways: first, in areas occupied by Han Chinese, the Qing government continued to employ the version of centralized administration *(junxian)* used during the Ming dynasty. In these areas, the central government held absolute authority, but this authority did not penetrate into the foundational level of society, as patrilineal clans and rural gentry continued to play extremely important roles throughout the Qing.[23] Second, during the Qing, the order of subordination and relationship of lord and vassal *(chenfu guanxi)* between the emperor on the one hand and Mongolia, Tibet, Xinjiang, and southwestern tribal states on the other was established within a multicentered framework of power, in which the former (the emperor) had no right to interfere directly in the latter's internal affairs. At the same time, the latter could maintain their own unique laws, religious faiths, and right to self-determination. The disintegration of the patrilineal clans and rural gentry is even more closely related to the Taiping Rebellion and modern nation-building movements in the nineteenth century. At the same time, three major factors contributed to changes in power relations between the central state and ethnic minority populations: first, in the process of facing external threats (such as those from Russia) and internal rebellions (such as the Revolt of the Three Feudatories [1673–1681] and the subsequent establishment of "regular" administrative regimes in non-Han areas [*gaitu guoliu*]), the empire attempted to use a variety of institutions to take back the autonomy held by the various outer regions. Second, with the development of large-scale intermingling of Manchu banner groups with Han Chinese and combinations of ethnic groups living among one another, the tensions that resulted from diverse sets of laws and institutions working alongside and against one another became a source of inequality for constituencies within the empire, and thus imperial declarations intended to secure the dynasty's legitimacy (such as "the unity of Manchu and Han") became the slogans used by the Han and other peoples to demand equal status. (Arguments for the relativization of foreign/Chinese differences and for ignoring inner/outer distinctions were in fact appeals for equality from the perspective of identity politics.) Third, beginning with the final years of the eighteenth century, European maritime hegemony and the opium trade began to intrude on the Qing economy and society, exerting serious pressure on the coastal regions. To bring in greater tax receipts and to stabilize the border regions, the Qing government began to expand the provincial government system used in the core regions to what had originally been tribute areas, thus creating a new trend toward centralizing power within the empire. In 1820, for example, Gong Zizhen wrote a memorial recommending the establishment of a seat of provincial government in the Western Territories (Xiyu, now Xinjiang), but, because the calligraphy of the document was unacceptable, it was not read by the emperor. Half a century later, however, this recommendation was finally put into action. We can understand this recommendation in the following ways. First, the system of provincial government insured that the central government could allow outward migration from the inner provinces to proceed without interference and thereby provide human power and resources that could resist the Russian Empire's eastward expansion. Second, the system of provincial government opened and strengthened the central government's direct channels of administration of the Western Territories, providing the state with institutional guarantees of greater tax collection from these areas, thereby ameliorating some of the central government's fiscal problems that began in the late eighteenth century as a result of the rapidly expanding opium trade. Third, European maritime hegemony went hand in hand with smuggling, and China needed to find another route to the outside other than southeastern maritime routes, and the Western Territories provided the necessary trade route to India.[24]

Geographical studies (*yudi xue*) of the northeastern territories from the first half of the nineteenth century responded to processes of Qing empire-building projects and to Russia's eastward expansion. At the same time, they also radically altered the ideas that the gentry had commonly held about China since the Ming dynasty, redefining the meaning of both "China" and the border regions. It is worth noting that much of the material contained under an entry titled "Foreign Customs" (*waiguo fengsu*) in the encyclopedic *Daily Accumulation of Knowledge* (*Ri zhi lu*) by Gu Yanwu had already by Gu's time become an organic part of imperial geography. The revival in geographical studies by Han gentry elites in this period was intrinsically related to the strategic considerations put forward by Gong Zizhen that I discussed earlier. The contents of these geographical studies went far beyond contemporary practices of geography (now called *dilixue* in Chinese). These geographical studies discussed aspects of the border regions such as language, religion, customs, population, irrigation, and other resource issues. In the early part of the Qing dynasty, Han gentry elites were unable to gain passage into northwestern and northeastern regions of the empire, and thus the majority of these elites remained accustomed to ideas about China that were formed during the Ming dynasty. Once the legitimacy of the empire was recognized, however, ideas of the relative nature of differences between Chinese and foreigners gradually moved from questions of identity into ideas about geography and place. Relationships between the center and the local and China and the foreign represented the internal forces behind these geographical studies. As early as 1689, the Qing court and the czar of Russia signed the Treaty of Nerchinsk, which was followed in the Yongzheng era (1722–1735) by the Treaty of Kyakhta (1727). These treaties involved drawing borders, developing mutual trade, and addressing questions related to movements of peoples living in border regions and jurisdiction over them. To create territorial treaties that could be mutually recognized by both parties, the Kangxi emperor invited European missionaries to assist in the drawing of the boundaries using advanced cartographic technologies, creating treaties with formal texts in Latin script and copies in Manchu and Russian. Issues of war and peace that were brought about by imperial expansion played an important role in the establishment of these boundaries, and also indicated that the boundaries that later served as markers of differences between the early empire and the nation-state were in fact created by competition between empires.

If geographical studies of the northwestern regions were the product of geographical relations produced by imperial expansion, then the emergence of an image of the world centered around the oceans would place China among the many "maritime states" *(haiguo)*. The trade in opium and especially the outbreak of the Opium Wars led the focus of geographical studies to shift from the Northwest to the southeastern coastal regions, Southeast Asia, and Europe. From the work of Xu Jiyu (1795–1873) onward, the project imagined by Lin Zexu (1785–1850) and completed by Wei Yuan in the *Gazetteer of the Maritime States (Haiguo tuzhi)* collected a wide variety of maps and information that could be brought together at that time. The *Gazetteer* not only established an extremely rich and complete view of the world and its historical context but also offered explanations of global power relations in terms of politics and economics. The major contributions of this work are as follows: first, Wei Yuan accurately calculated the extent of the opium trade and the trade deficits that it created for the Qing dynasty, explaining how eighteenth-century England's Industrial Revolution resulted in a global transformation of trade relations. Wei also illustrated the role played by the operations of the East India Company and the dominant position of England's naval power throughout this process of industrialization, thereby offering an overall understanding of the new global power relations that were forming at that time, the forces behind them, and the challenges that China faced. The basic plan Wei Yuan offered was to bring together the power of the court and private interests to increase development of shipbuilding, navigation, and naval power, linking military defense and industry together and, at the same time, reorganizing government institutions of management by addressing the needs of both the military and commerce. This process of military industrialization was an important precondition for state building throughout the late Qing. Second, in the areas of thought and knowledge, Wei Yuan argued for a revival of the maritime communication routes of the Song and Ming dynasties, redrawing the map of the world in a way that focused on maritime networks, and emphasized the importance of Southeast Asia in China's tribute system. Because of its conflict with Koxinga (Zheng Chenggong, 1624–1662) and the blockade on Taiwan, the early-Qing state implemented a "sea ban," a prohibition on private maritime navigation. The Kangxi emperor, however, never gave up on efforts to promote maritime trade. A large number of events demonstrate that in the seventeenth and eighteenth centuries the Qing dynasty signed treaties and developed tribute relations with neighboring states and with European states to form extremely complex economic and cultural relationships.[25] Beginning in the late Qianlong era, the Qing dynasty's limitations on trade grew ever stricter,[26] but the emergence of these policies cannot simply be attributed to an attitude of closed-off conservatism. They were, rather, a response to new international trade relations: the Industrial Revolution in eighteenth-century England resulted in a global transformation in trade relations, and the East India Company and the dominant position of England's naval power became defining factors of this era. As the crisis grew ever deeper, Wei Yuan made this discovery: closed borders and limited trade could not protect China's most important interests. The Great Qing had to undertake reforms that moved in the direction of both opening up and self-protection in economic, military, and political matters.

Modern sovereignty is a product of a new kind of international relations of recognition. Because the treaty system assumed sovereignty based on formal equality, nationalism also used this assumption to resist unequal relations of the imperial era. Trade and diplomatic relations between empires fell under the name of the "tribute system"; the concept of "tribute" also implied a hierarchy. For this reason, then, people frequently placed the tribute system in opposition to the treaty system. However, if we look briefly at a number of bilateral treaties from before 1840, we will see that the tribute system not only addressed issues related to trade, but also worked in ways that were parallel (and not opposed) to the treaty system. Under the relations of the tribute system, different subjects had different ways of construing tribute relations, and thus the system of hierarchies within tribute ritual also produced actual equality through respective statements of position. The failure of the tribute/treaty system was the result of new-style international relations and structures of hegemony, not the victory of sovereignty and formal equality over the inequality of the tribute system model. Unlike the Treaty of Nerchinsk of 1689 and a number of subsequent bilateral treaties signed with European states, the treaties signed following the Opium Wars no longer allowed the Qing dynasty to maintain any notion of the tribute system, yet maintained the recognition of Qing sovereignty found in earlier treaties. European colonialists painted the conflict between the Qing dynasty and the European powers as the result of the Qing's refusal to engage in free trade and the court's ignorance of international law, but herein lies a historical irony: to allow the Qing dynasty to legally sign an unequal treaty, the Qing had to be granted formal equality and sovereignty under European international law, and yet the treaties established under the shroud of European international law were even more unfair than the treaties from the era of the tribute system. In the long process that stretched from the seventeenth century through the nineteenth century, the mutually recognized sovereignty of European states was limited to those European "Christian states." From the Opium Wars on, however, European states had to sign unequal treaties with autonomous entities from outside of Europe that also possessed formal equality, bringing the Qing dynasty into the system of treaties led by European states. Even if European colonial nations continued to use the complexities of China's internal relations— such as ethnic relations and central/regional relations—to their own advantage, the concept of the sovereign state clearly took for granted the existence of a unified, sovereign authority; that is, the concept of the sovereign state assumes that the nation-state possesses the sole source of sovereignty, and that other nation-states must take this sole sovereign authority as any given nation's only political authority. The unitary nature of sovereignty was a product of the history of the European absolutist state; it broke apart the multipolar structure of power of the feudal era and provided a historical basis for the formation of the nation-state. When this concept of sovereignty, based on unified authority, formal equality, and recognition between states made its way to China and other parts of the world, it worked to reduce the traditional tribute system and its model for relations of inner and outer to a secondary model unsuited to the times. From another direction, then, these developments helped to push the Qing empire toward a transformation into a unified sovereign state. The process of the translation and introduction of Henry Wheaton's *Elements of International Law* (called *Wanguo gongfa* or *Laws of the Myriad States* in Chinese) was an important milestone and outcome of this process of transformation toward sovereignty.[27]

In this historical context, gentry elites and more sensitive officials in court finally brought a new perception of the world situation into the dynasty's view of itself. Combining European scientific and political knowledge with Confucian ideas, they proposed for China a new set of inner/outer relations, and drew from the *Spring and Autumn Annals, Rites of Zhou (Zhou li)*, and other classic texts to find ideas concerning international law and to bring a global outlook to traditional geographical studies. During this time it was popular to describe the competition between nation-states in terms of the "contending states" of the Warring States period. In this context, the use of the *Spring and Autumn Annals* and the *Rites of Zhou* as early models of international law implied a certain reverence for the Western Zhou and Spring and Autumn eras: the Warring States period was a time that lacked ritual and trust and relied on subterfuge and violence, as in the famous stories of Zhang Yi's multiple deceptions of the King of Chu.[28] By comparison, even if international relations in the Spring and Autumn era often led to war, standards of honesty and trust were maintained, as when Duke Wen of Jin (697–628 B.C.E.) withdrew his troops after ten days of making war on the Kingdom of Yuan.[29] This is a kind of method for extending Confucian principles into international relations. Kang Youwei, shocked by the deep crisis in the tribute system, saw the advent of the era of "contending powers" as a way to renew the sovereign state based on the power and authority of the emperor. Kang's emphasis on the centrality of the emperor not only reflected his direct political motivations toward the regency of the Empress Cixi, but, more important, also took into account the symbolic problems of Chinese sovereignty: the power of the emperor represented all of the peoples and territories in the empire. If the power of the emperor were to collapse, then a Chinese identity based on Confucianism would be replaced by a European-style national identity, and thus the breakup of the empire would become unavoidable. Kang Youwei's reform proposals were predicated on the symbolic nature of the power of the emperor. Kang called for transforming the empire directly into a sovereign unit, using reforms of both central and local government institutions to support this new sovereign form.[30] Late Qing revolutionaries may have used anti-Manchu slogans in support of a Han nationalism, but the 1911 revolution resulted in a republican political structure of "Five Nations Under One Union" that exercised national self-determination in foreign affairs while, in the domestic realm, practiced equality among national/ethnic groups within its borders. The republican proposals of the revolutionary parties differed from the model of constitutional monarchy offered by Kang Youwei, but there was very little space between them when it came to the question of directly transforming the empire into a sovereign state. For the new Republic, political autonomy referred first and foremost to the autonomy of the people in opposition to the power of the emperor and aristocratic institutions; secondary to this was the autonomy of the state in relation to European colonialism. Important differences can be seen between this republican model of autonomy and the model of the nation-state that was produced in response to the forms of government of European empires. In structural terms, there are obvious continuities between China as a modern, sovereign state and the Chinese empire. Thus the founders of the Republic of China could use the continuity of "orthodoxy" *(daotong)* to provide the new state with historical legitimacy. Concentration of power in the central state and the unification of political structure was a result of both internal and external pressures, and was also a product of the relations of recognition among sole sovereign authorities in the new system of nation-states. The hegemony of colonialism, relations of mutual recognition under European international law, and internal reforms undertaken by the Qing dynasty all worked from different directions to create a definition for "China" as a sovereign state.

5. EMPIRE BUILDING, STATE BUILDING, AND THE TENDENCY TOWARD CENTRALIZATION OF POWER

We see many overlapping processes and points of intersection between trends toward centralization of power in Qing-dynasty empire-building projects and late-Qing state building. Two of the most important among these are a model for national identity based on the rights of citizens and a political structure based on unitary sovereign authority. We may see these two items as clear boundaries between empire-building projects and state-building projects. First, whereas the unity of the early period of the dynasty recognized multiple political structures and cultural identities of the many nationalities and regions within its borders, state-building projects from the late Qing onward worked to bring multiple social institutions into a relatively unitary political structure. The diverse centers of power within the empire and other elements of autonomy were gradually weakened and eliminated during the process of transforming the empire into a sovereign state. All social reforms that took place from the Opium Wars onward focused on a single goal: reestablishing a strong state with centralized authority, even if that meant destroying those elements within old institutions that contradicted the idea of this strong central state. When seen in terms of modernization, this centralization is a crowning achievement of historical progress because without centralized power, a state cannot achieve the goal of industrialization, resist imperialism and foreign invasions, or form agency/autonomy within society. At the same time, however, this progress also gives rise to a new crisis because traditional dynasties have never worked completely like modern societies in rejecting all aspects of local autonomy and wiping out existing social structures. The modern revolution wiped out the Eight Banners system of the Manchus and Mongolians, the Kashag system of the Tibetans, the social institutions of southeastern tribal societies, local institutions in Xinjiang, the rural patriarchal clan system, as well as all of the various forms of autonomy that were held within them, thus providing the conditions for the promotion of state-building projects. It is particularly worth noting that late-Qing political reforms included reforms concerning separation of powers and local autonomy, but this separation of powers and bestowal of local autonomy assumed a fundamental unification of institutions and unified sovereignty, and thus was quite different from the pluralist approach to institutions and laws taken during the imperial era. In the tribute system, the various regions and nationalities were not brought under a singular, unified political structure; but the core of early modern state building is to form a unified political structure. Elie Kedourie's discussion of nationalism in central Europe is helpful to our current discussion:

> The states which resulted from the application of the principle of self-determination are as full of anomalies and mixed areas as the heterogeneous empires they have replaced. In a nation-state, however, the issues raised by the presence of heterogeneous groups are much more acute than in an empire. If, in a mixed area, one group makes good a territorial claim and establishes a nation-state, other groups will feel threatened and resentful. For them to be ruled by one group claiming to rule in its own national territory is worse

than to be governed by an empire which does not base its title to rule on national grounds. To an imperial government the groups in a mixed area are all equally entitled to some consideration, to a national government they are a foreign body in the state to be either assimilated or rejected. The national state claims to treat all citizens as equal members of the nation, but this fair-sounding principle only serves to disguise the tyranny of one group over another.[31]

China's movements of national self-determination faced similar questions, and thus Chinese identity and state building always faced the problem of how to handle the property and wealth inherited from the imperial era according to principles of equality among nationalities in order to overcome the problems of inequality among nationalities brought on by the unified sovereignty of the nation-state. China's system of autonomous regions combined the concept of national sovereignty and the leftovers of the imperial system; the granting of autonomous power and application of principles of national equality, then, are inextricably linked.

Second, the trend toward centralization of power in the modern nation-state was dependent on the production of a new model of identity, one that went beyond family, region, and ethnicity. The concept of the citizen or national citizen (*guomin*) and its legal status worked to liberate the individual from the power of local relationships found in the family, religion, or clan, and to organize the individual directly into a network guided by the state:

> The nationalism of the national state is bureaucratic as well as civic. For the national state is institutionalized, and represented, through the bureaucracy and its organs in their relations with its citizens. So the bureaucracy and its staff increasingly forms the locus of the nationalism of the national state, not simply in terms of the material and status interests of the incumbents of bureaucratic offices, but in terms of the power and unity and interests of the national state itself.[32]

The power of the patriarchal clan system expanded greatly during the Qing dynasty, becoming a structure of shared power alongside that of the central government and bureaucratic institutions. To solidify the institutions of the Manchu Qing dynasty, a great deal of support was given to clan institutions during the reigns of the Kangxi, Yongzheng, and Qianlong emperors; in later years, these clan institutions even took the place of some local governmental functions. In the eighteenth century, clan power continued to expand, to such an extent that some clans competed with local governments for power and even exceeded the limits that had been placed on them by the state. To even out the situation, the Qianlong emperor placed limits on clan power, even punishing some clan leaders who had overstepped their powers and privately ordered executions of members of their own groups. The central government, however, never thoroughly dissolved clan institutions. During the late-Qing period, the reformist factions, approaching the question from the point of view of separation of powers, equated China's clan system with European civil society, arguing that it constituted an institution for the separation of power and a social basis for the self-management of society. However, one of the major functions of modern Chinese revolutions was to liberate the peasantry from bloodline relations and local relations, transforming them into a key revolutionary force, the "citizens" of the state, and cheap labor power for the process of urban industrialization. In this sense, the "citizen" and his or her rights have a direct relationship to the state's identity and its plans for industrialization: his or her main mission and duty is not a mission or duty for the family or community, but for the nation or state. According to Anthony D. Smith,

> Not only ethnic but also civic nationalisms may demand the eradication of minority cultures and communities qua communities, on the common assumption, shared by Marxists and liberals, not just of equality through uniformity, but that "high cultures" and "great nations" are necessarily of greater value than "low" cultures and small nations or *ethnies* [ethnic communities]. So the pedagogical narrative of Western democracies turns out to be every bit as demanding and rigorous—and in practice ethnically one-sided—as are those of non-Western authoritarian state-nations, since it assumes the assimilation of ethnic minorities within the borders of the national

state through acculturation to a hegemonic majority ethnic culture. The civic equality of co-nationals destroys all associations and bodies that stand between the citizen and the state, and the ideology of civic nationalism relegates the customary and vernacular to the margins of society, to the family and folklore. In doing so, it also delegitimizes and devalues the ethnic cultures of resident minorities and immigrants alike, and does so consciously and deliberately.[33]

For these reasons, modern state-building movements neither developed according to ideas about local, shared power found in the late Ming or late Qing nor progressed according to the framework of empire building used during the Qing dynasty in the seventeenth and eighteenth centuries. Rather, they moved in the direction of eliminating foundational social organizations and institutional diversity. The nationalists of the 1911 revolution, the enlightenment intellectuals of the May Fourth era, and Mao Zedong, leader of the Chinese Communist Revolution, all held extremely similar views on the power of local clans: they all saw them as the most important leftover of China's "feudal" tradition, the greatest obstacle to the social mobilization of China (the "heap of loose sand" referred to by Sun Yat-sen), and the basic target of the Chinese revolution. Under the banner of national equality, citizens' rights, and legitimacy of the people's state, the modern nation-state works in the name of "revolution," "liberation," and "legal rights" to reorganize the individual into collective institutions guided by the state, thereby granting the modern nation-state more direct power to control the individual. When people trace the sources of modern authoritarianism to imperial traditions, they ignore very important differences between patterns of social organization found in modern centralized power and in the modes of social control from the imperial era. If we depart from the complex historical relations of inner and outer described earlier, if we depart from military and trade relations, and if we depart from questions related to the global expansion of the European system of state sovereignty, then we cannot explain trends relating to the centralization of power in the modern state and social conditions relating to the convergence of administrative structures.

About a century and a half ago, Alexis de Tocqueville analyzed a variety of documents and writings and, looking at then-contemporary France, found to his surprise that many of the feelings that originated in the French revolution, many of the ideas that came from the French Revolution, and many of the customs and attitudes that came from the French Revolution in fact came out of the old French society. Tocqueville maintained resolutely that modern France's centralized system of power was not a result of the revolution, but a product of the *ancien régime,* and, in fact, the only part of the *ancien régime* that had been preserved in the political system since the revolution because only this aspect of the *ancien régime* was sufficient to handle the new society established by the revolution.[34] In a certain sense, a consequence of the late-Qing revolutions for political institutions was to revive, within the territory and population structure of the Qing empire, a state structure based on the system of centralized administration (*junxian zhi*) from the Song and Ming dynasties, and thus, working in accordance with the process of institutional convergence that occurred as a result of Qing empire-building projects, to expand the system of centralized administration into an imperial administrative structure. The Chinese revolution did not follow a European model in which states that had originally been monarchies broke away from imperial rule, but rather formed a unified sovereign state by merging together nation and state on the foundation of the old Qing dynasty. Sun Yat-sen's nationalism was characterized by its dual emphasis on both seeking national self-determination through resistance to foreign incursions and effecting equality among different nationalities: in the process of the disintegration of the old imperial system, he did not encourage each national group to form its own independent political structure, but rather called for the transformation of the Qing political structure through its current geography and population, eliminating special powers accorded to certain nationalities and leading this new entity to form into a sovereign unit in the global system of nation-states. From the late-Qing revolutions until the founding of the People's Republic of China in 1949, despite the many events that occurred during these years— seizures of territory, endless military campaigns, economic devastation, foreign invasions, and civil war—China, in the end, reappeared before the world in the form of an independent sovereign state that drew legitimacy from the people, yet one whose territorial borders and population scarcely differed from the Qing dynasty. The Chinese revolution has generally been seen as a national revolution, but the true consequence of this national revolution has been to transform China from an empire into a sovereign state within the nation-state system.

Why, however, did this new society require and even expand on the aspects of centralized power found in the *ancien régime?* Not much earlier than Tocqueville, Marx, writing in 1848, also assessed the changes that had taken place in France. Like Tocqueville, he also sighed with regret: "The tradition of all the dead generations weighs like a nightmare on the brain of the living." At the same time, however, he also reminded us: "Consideration of this conjuring up of the dead of world history reveals at once a salient difference."[35] When they reappear, the spirits of history respond to completely different voices from history, playing historical roles that are utterly different from those that they played when they first appeared. For historians, it is not productive to conclude that a society's predicament is simply predestined by its traditions and history; it is more useful to ask where one might find the forces that have created its new historical trajectories. Why are some elements completely wiped out, while others reappear in new guises? When theories of the legitimacy of the nation-state lay all of the blame for past evils at the door of "empire," what, then, are the real historical forces that have evaded our perspective? Which of those mechanisms that continuously lead to disaster have become almost commonplace, completely naturalized orders? If the nation-state is the "natural state" of capitalism, then the core of this new state-building project develops around developmental capitalism or the logic of modernization. Historical capitalism and state socialism are not fundamentally different from one another in the ways they undertake capital accumulation, division of labor, and organization of production under the nation-state form so as to establish a national economy that can participate in international competition. Indeed, as Lenin pointed out in response to Sun Yat-sen's project to create a form of democracy and socialism that would overcome and exceed the limits of capitalism, "the irony of history [is that] Narodnism, in the name of the 'struggle against capitalism' in agriculture, advocates an agrarian program which, if fully realized, would mean the *most* rapid development of capitalism in agriculture."[36] But it was this anticapitalist agenda that provided developmental capitalism with its most effective tools. This new model of Asian nationalism was, first and foremost, very closely linked with the new divisions of labor that emerged under the conditions of capitalism and their impact on existing social relations. The accumulation of capital required the restructuring of existing relations in the countryside and population patterns, thereby creating the conditions for industrialization. All of this implies that nation-state building must result in the formation of new kinds of hierarchies: cities versus countryside, urban population versus rural population, the newly drawn class structure, and the unequal system of political power that formed through appeals to legitimacy that were based on democracy and equality.

The modern state and capitalism require complex and effective institutions and legal structures, and thus institutional reform and the creation of legal systems occupied all reform movements from the late Qing onward. An important aspect in the development of modern thought was the focus on institutions throughout various movements. In his discussion of nations and nationalism, Ernest Gellner concluded:

> The general emergence of modernity hinged on the erosion of the multiple petty binding local organizations and their replacement by mobile, anonymous, literate, identity-conferring cultures. It is this generalized condition which made nationalism normative and pervasive; and this is not contradicted by the occasional superimposition of both of these types of loyalty, the occasional use of kin links for a kind of interstitial, parasitic and partial adaptation to the new order. Modern industry can be paternalistic, and nepotistic at the top; but it cannot recruit its productive units on the basis of kin or territorial principles, as tribal society had done. . . . Modern societies are always and inevitably centralized, in the sense that the maintenance of order is the task of one agency or group of agencies, and not dispersed throughout the society. The complex division of labor, the complementarity and interdependence and the constant mobility:

all these factors prevent citizens from doubling up as producers and participants in violence. There are societies—notably some pastoral ones—where this is feasible: the shepherd is simultaneously the soldier, and often also the senator, jurist, and minstrel of his tribe. The entire culture, or very nearly, of the whole society seems encapsulated in each individual rather than distributed among them in different forms, and the society seems to refrain from specialization, at least in its male half, to a very remarkable degree. The few specialists whom this kind of society tolerates it also despises.[37]

In both the early Qing and late Qing, Chinese thought saw two periods in which Song-Ming neo-Confucianism underwent severe criticism. The former led to the rise of statecraft learning and studies of the classics (*jingxue*), whereas the latter paved the way for the transmission of a wide variety of types of political thought and technical knowledge. For this reason, late-Qing thought also often appealed to ideas about ethnicity and theories of practice found in early-Qing statecraft learning, providing resources for national identity and political reform. If we compare Gu Yanwu and Kang Youwei, however, we see that although both men used Confucianism as the general background for their model of an ideal society: the former laid his foundation on rites and music; the latter based his argument on the question of institutions. Gu Yanwu emphasized the implicit connections between local customs, practices, and autonomous traditions and the category of "China," explaining this core belief in his call to "suffuse the spirit of the system of enfeoffment within the system of centralized administration." Kang Youwei, however, emphasized a state structure centered on the emperor and worked to establish a constitution, parliament, and Western-style administrative institutions and legal systems as the fundamentals for any state-building project.[38] One of the most important aspects of late-Qing thought is the large-scale introduction, translation, and interpretation of Western knowledge, as well as efforts to link the mapping of this knowledge with the building of state institutions. Even if the legal traditions of centralized administration (*junxian*) provided a complete framework, the direction of reform was always moving toward remaking this framework completely into a political structure suited to the unified sovereign state and into a legal/power system that could spur on the development of capitalism.[39]

When the legitimacy and authority of the state/social system became a fundamental issue for late-Qing thought, the critical reflections that were directed at constraints created by this system appealed to new standards: from within the framework of New Text scholarship, Kang Youwei drew from a variety of strands of Western political thought to form a theory of state building that drew from earlier notions dynastic grand unification. At the same time, however, he also combined Confucian and Buddhist ideas with European utopian thought and, together with a cosmology of science, created a vision of a world of a grand unity (da tong) that would eliminate the nation-state and other units of society. Yan Fu translated a number of major works by writers such as Herbert Spencer, John Stuart Mill, Montesquieu, and Thomas Huxley on theories of the state, law, economic theory, social theory, science, and history, but also combined Laozi's doctrine of nonaction (wuwei) with European liberal ideals (especially as they related to the ideas about the rights of the individual) to keep the learning that he believed led to national wealth and power from forming into systemic restraints.[40] Liang Qichao argued that the state was an organic entity and advocated an open nationalism (da minzu zhuyi), but also unearthed ideas about individual autonomy and local autonomy from schools of thought based in the work of Wang Yangming and in European philosophers such as Immanuel Kant. At the same time, Liang also attempted to bring moral elements into evolutionary thought, reconciling the sharp contradictions between science and ethics.[41] Zhang Taiyan used Old Text classicism to draw together strands of Western nationalist thought, providing a genealogy of knowledge to support the establishment of a kind of Han nationalist identity. At the same time, through his readings of Yogācāra (consciousness-only) Buddhism and works by German philosophers such as Johann Gottlieb Fichte (1762–1814) and Friedrich Nietzsche (1844–1900), Zhang also unearthed ideas that radically opposed the dominance of state and society over the individual, ultimately reaching a point where he used Zhuangzi's "On Equalizing Things" (Qi wu lun) and Buddhist philosophy to structure a kind of negative utopia directed against the system of modernity that had already appeared in Europe and that was taking hold in China.[42] Such paradoxical, conflicting elements appeared at all levels in the many divergent areas of intellectual history of the period; it is for this reason that they provided extremely important resources for the establishment of modern Chinese identity and for self-reflection on that process.

From the late Qing onward, social movements centered on state reform combined Chinese identities formed during the Qing dynasty, geographical relationships formed during processes of imperial expansion and the knowledge that developed from these geographical relationships, and international relationships of recognition, placing all of these into modernization projects of state building and economic reorganization and into temporally marked paths of development. The decline of the dynasty provided the conditions for the republican political form to gain legitimacy, but major elements of the identities and institutional structures of the imperial era were also reorganized into the political identities and political structures of the Republican era. From the large-scale development of urban print culture (media, literature, textbooks, etc.) to the outward flow and expansion of power from the city to the countryside during the wartime era, national identity took a path of many twists and turns. Capitalism and the global relations it creates are the most important forces behind newly emergent state identities and forms of sovereignty, and also give rise to the most important forces behind the crises and transformations that occur in national identity and forms of sovereignty. The most important phenomenon in twentieth-century world history—the Chinese revolution and the ideology that came from it— took shape in this crisis and transformation; it is this process of revolution that transformed traditional forms of identity, restructured forms of state sovereignty, created new political-social structures and forms of identity, and provided basic historical conditions for a variety of different political agendas. However, with the disintegration of the Soviet Union and the Eastern European system, China's adoption of the policy of reform and opening up, and historical changes in other regions, political concepts formed in the nineteenth and twentieth centuries such as colonialism, imperialism, and nationalism were reorganized or absorbed into a developmentalist framework represented by the general term "globalization."

If we say this concept largely represents the penetration of the global economy into every corner of the world, then the application of another piece of imperial terminology—the concept represented by the word "empire"—attempts to describe the political form of this world economy.[43] There is an important difference between this concept of "empire" and the traditional concept of empire, to the extent that some doubt the usefulness of the new concept. If we are indeed going to discuss its outlines, then it seems that this term as it is used in this instance has a conceptual relationship that is closer to imperialism as a specific form of capitalism. In terms of the world economy, globalization has not produced a political structure as clearly defined as those found in early empires, and thus cannot be discussed as part of the same category as traditional empires. However, one point can still be determined: regardless of the many different opinions about what terms should be used to describe contemporary forms of global rule, it is widely believed that the forms of sovereignty, models of identity, and global relations created by modern revolutions are currently facing a deep and wide-ranging crisis. Therefore, efforts to reinterpret forms of sovereignty and the crises of legitimacy produced by the revolutions and the historical changes of the nineteenth and twentieth centuries play an important function for understanding changes in the contemporary world and what lies ahead. *The Rise of Modern Chinese Thought* takes on a few basic questions in modern thought and the legitimation of knowledge, but does not undertake a direct and open discussion of the Chinese revolution and movements of social resistance in earlier periods. I hope that in later scholarly work I will be able to undertake a more thorough analysis of this unavoidable historical question.

*   *   *

After explaining my basic line of thought, I would like to briefly sketch out the basic structure of *The Rise of Modern Chinese Thought*. This book is divided into four parts: "Principle and Things"; "Empire and Nation-State"; "Universal Principle and Opposition to Universal Principle"; and "The Community of Scientific Language and Its Fragmentation." From the perspective of intellectual history, I ask the following questions:

What are the historical forces that formed from the worldview of Heavenly Principle *(tianli)* as it took shape during the Northern Song dynasty? Exactly what is the relationship between empire-building projects of the Qing dynasty and state-building projects in modern China? What kinds of intellectual resources can be found in the complicated attitude toward modernity found in late Qing thought? How were modern China's institutions and systems of knowledge established? By taking changes in Chinese thought and society as a starting point for these larger questions, this research offers a historical understanding of "China," "China's modern" *(Zhongguode xiandai),* and the modern significance of Chinese thought, as well as an understanding of the problem of modernity. Concepts such as "China," "modern China," "Chinese thought," or "modernity" are historical categories in historical narrative; any means of naturalizing these concepts comes to bear on and limit the depth of our inquiry. As in this book's discussion of "Heavenly Principle," no concept or category can be sheltered by a natural category, and even Heavenly Principle and nature *(ziran)* itself must be subjected to historical analysis. The meaning of historical analysis, however, is not to empty out the historical meaning of these concepts; indeed, this book's analysis of Chinese thought begins precisely with the processes surrounding the emergence of these concepts. From this reflexive outlook, my research and discussion largely covers the following areas: first, the Confucian intellectual tradition and its transformation; second, within a multinational dynasty, how Confucianism manages relations among different ethnic groups and defines the meaning of "China" *(Zhongguo);* third, the relationship that formed between the Qing imperial tradition and the tradition of the modern state, and their models of inner/outer relations; and fourth, nationalism and the formation of modern knowledge and institutions. In the framework of this book, all of these questions are held together and analyzed in terms of intellectual history—especially the transformation of Confucianism. I did not set out to write a flat chronology of events or to address questions of intellectual history according to the methods of the history of concepts *(Begriffsgeschichte)* or philosophy. My method is to discuss people, events, and problems from intellectual history within a larger, fixed structure of questions, and then to use these questions to guide the entire study. Thus we have both general analysis and discussion of specific cases: chapters 1 and 2 of Part 1 undertake a general analysis of Song and Ming neo-Confucianism (but largely concentrate on the establishment of the concept of Heavenly Principle), whereas other chapters deal with individual cases, analyzing texts, individuals, and historical discourses to expand on the major questions that concern me. Structuring the chapters around ideas and individuals also serves the goals of the entire book, providing an opportunity to demonstrate as much as possible the circumstances and complexity of each specific idea or individual while avoiding an overarching narrative that simply forces these ideas and individuals to serve my purposes. For these reasons, the full historical arguments of the chapters can only be grasped when they are placed in the context of the larger narrative; at the same time, however, the analyses can stand relatively independently. Both Part 1 and Part 2 of *The Rise of Modern Chinese Thought* take shape naturally through the historical narrative, but also consider the major questions discussed by one another, as well as the connections and differences between them. For those readers who do not have time to read the entire book, it is entirely workable to read only those relevant portions of their choice. The current work, the Introduction *(Daolun)*, largely consists of an explanation of the major arguments in Part 1, whereas most of the summations of Part 2 are gathered in the Conclusion *(Zongjie)*. The two, however, compose a whole, and the tension between them is a manifestation of that wholeness. Because the process of writing this book stretched out over ten years, I am already unable to sketch out the complete context of my theoretical considerations and how they have changed—this is something that still needs to be addressed.

Notes

TRANSLATOR'S INTRODUCTION

1. Three volumes of Wang's work have already been translated into English: *The Politics of Imagining Asia,* ed. Theodore Huters (Cambridge, MA: Harvard University Press, 2011); *The End of the Revolution: China and the Limits of Modernity* (London: Verso, 2009); and *China's New Order: Society, Politics, and Economy in Transition,* ed. Theodore Huters and Rebecca Karl (Cambridge, MA: Harvard University Press, 2006). For an important early interview in English, see Wang Hui, "Fire at the Castle Gate," *New Left Review* 6 (November–December 2000): 68–99.

2. Zhang Yongle has produced the most detailed discussion of the full contents of Wang's study. See Zhang Yongle, "The Future of the Past: On Wang Hui's *Rise of Modern Chinese Thought,*" *New Left Review* 62 (March–April 2010): 47–83. Other discussions and reviews include Claudia Pozzana and Alessandro Russo, "Circumstances, Politics, and History: Reading Notes on Wang Hui's 'General Introduction' to *The Rise of Modern Chinese Thought,*" trans. Michaela Duranti, *positions: east asia cultures critique* 20, no. 1 (2012): 307–27; Philip C. C. Huang, "In Search of Chinese Modernity: Wang Hui's *The Rise of Modern Chinese Thought,*" *Modern China* 34, no. 3 (2008): 396–404; Wang Ban, "Discovering Enlightenment in Chinese History: *The Rise of Modern Chinese Thought,*" *boundary 2* 34 (2007): 217–38; Viren Murthy, "Modernity against Modernity: Wang Hui's Critical History of Chinese Thought," *Modern Intellectual History* 3, no. 1 (2006): 137–65.

147

For essays and interviews in English by Wang Hui that speak directly to *The Rise of Modern Chinese Thought*, see "A Dialogue on *The Rise of Modern Chinese Thought*," trans. Tani Barlow, *positions: east asia cultures critique* 20, no. 1 (2012): 287–306; Wang Hui, "How to Explain 'China' and Its 'Modernity': Rethinking the *Rise of Modern Chinese Thought*," trans. Wang Yang, in Huters, ed., *The Politics of Imagining Asia*, 63–94; Wang Hui, "Rethinking *The Rise of Modern Chinese Thought*," trans. Audrea Lim, in *The End of the Revolution*, 105–38; "The Liberation of the Object and the Interrogation of Modernity," *Modern China* 34, no. 1 (2008): 114–40. Translations of the present text have already appeared in Italian and Japanese. See *Impero o Stato-Nazione? La modernità intellettuale in Cina*, trans. Gaia Perini (Milano: Academia Universa Press, 2009); *Kindai Chūgoku shisō no seisei*, trans. Ishii Tsuyoshi (Tokyo: Iwanami Shoten, 2011).

3. See "The 'Tibetan Question' East and West: Orientalism, Regional Ethnic Autonomy, and the Politics of Dignity," trans. Theodore Huters, in Huters, ed., *The Politics of Imagining Asia*, 136–227.

4. See Lydia Liu, *Translingual Practice: Literature, National Culture, and Translated Modernity, 1900–1937* (Stanford, CA: Stanford University Press, 1995).

5. Wang Hui, "Liberation of the Object," 126.

6. Wang Hui, *Xiandai Zhongguo sixiangde xingqi*, 2nd ed. (Beijing: Sanlian, 2008), 4: 1492. Translation borrowed from Murthy, "Modernity against Modernity," 137.

7. See Wang Hui, "The Fate of 'Mr. Science' in China: The Concept of Science and Its Application in Modern Chinese Thought," trans. Howard Y. F. Choy, *positions: east asia cultures critique* 3, no. 1 (Spring 1995): 1–68; Wang Hui, "On Scientism and Social Theory in Modern Chinese Thought," trans. Gloria Davies, in *Voicing Concerns: Contemporary Chinese Critical Inquiry*, ed. Gloria Davies (Lanham, MD: Rowman & Littlefield, 2001), 135–56. A useful earlier treatment is found in D. W. Y. Kwok, *Scientism in Chinese Thought, 1900–1950* (New Haven, CT: Yale University Press, 1965).

8. See Peter Zarrow, *After Empire: The Conceptual Transformation of the Chinese State, 1885–1924* (Stanford, CA: Stanford University Press, 2012), 95, 319–20.

9. See Heige'er [G. W. F. Hegel], *Lishi zhexue*, trans. Wang Zaoshi (rpt., Shanghai: Shanghai shudian, 2006).

10. Gloria Davies notes that this accusation is commonly made against so-called "New Left" thinkers (a category that Wang Hui himself refuses to recognize as accurate or adequate). See Davies, *Worrying about China: The Language of Chinese Critical Inquiry* (Cambridge, MA: Harvard University Press, 2007), 220–21.

11. For illuminating discussions on the problem of style in theoretical writing, see the essays collected in *Just Being Difficult? Academic Writing in the Public Arena,* ed. Jonathan Culler and Kevin Lamb (Stanford, CA: Stanford University Press, 2003).

CHINA FROM EMPIRE TO NATION-STATE

1. On the historical origins of the appellation *Zhongguo* [China], see Wang Ermin, "'Zhongguo' mingcheng suyuan jiqi jindai quanshi" [On the origins of the term *Zhongguo* and its modern interpretations], *Zhongguo jindai sixiang shi lun* [Discussions of modern Chinese history] (Beijing: Shehui kexue wenxian chubanshe, 2003), 370–400.

1. TWO NARRATIVES OF CHINA AND THEIR DERIVATIVE FORMS

1. Among the many works on intellectual history by Chinese Marxists, the richest and most impressive work can still be found in Hou Wailu, Zhao Jilun, Du Guoxiang, et al., *Zhongguo sixiang tongshi* [General history of Chinese thought] (Beijing: Renmin chubanshe, 1957).

2. See John K. Fairbank, *China: Tradition and Transformation* (Boston: Houghton Mifflin, 1989); Max Weber, *Konfuzianismus und Taoismus: Gesammelte Aufsätze zur Religionssoziologie* (Tübingen: Mohr, 1978); Joseph R. Levenson, *Confucian China and its Modern Fate* (Berkeley: University of California Press, 1968).

3. See Wang, *Rise of Modern Chinese Thought,* chapter 13. [These references point to chapters in the larger and still untranslated *Rise of Modern Chinese Thought (Xiandai Zhongguo sixiangde xingqi).*—Trans.]

4. See Paul A. Cohen, *Discovering History in China: American Historical Writing on the Recent Chinese Past* (New York: Columbia University Press, 1984). [The Chinese translation of this book was published by Zhonghua shuju in 1989 under the title *Zai Zhongguo faxian lishi—Zhongguo zhongxin guan zai Meiguode xingqi* (Discovering

history in China—the rise of China-centered history in the United States).—Trans.]

5. Naitō Konan, "Gaikuode Tang-Song shidai guan" [An overview of the Tang-Song era], in *Riben xuezhe yanjiu Zhongguo shi lunzhu xuanyi* [Selected translations of works on Chinese history by scholars from Japan] (Beijing: Zhonghua shuju, 1992), 1:10–18.

6. Miyazaki Ichisada, "Dongyangde jinshi," in *Riben xuezhe yanjiu Zhongguo shi lunzhu xuanyi,* 1:153–242.

7. Hamashita Takeshi, *Jindai Zhongguode guoji qiji—chaogong maoyi tixi yu jindai Yazhou jingji quan* [The turning point in modern Chinese international relations—the tribute trade system and the modern Asian economic sphere], trans. Zhu Yingui and Ouyang Fei (Beijing: Zhongguo shehui kexue chubanshe, 1999).

8. Andre Gunder Frank, *ReOrient: Global Economy in the Asian Age* (Berkeley: University of California Press, 1998).

9. Harold J. Berman, *Law and Revolution: The Formation of the Western Legal Tradition* (Cambridge, MA: Harvard University Press, 1983), 2–3.

10. Ibid., 4.

11. Most studies of the "sprouts of capitalism" are concentrated in the field of economic history. For representative works, see Xu Dixin and Wu Chengming, eds., *Zhongguo zibenzhuyi fazhan shi: Zhongguo zibenzhuyi mengya* [The development of capitalism in China: China's sprouts of capitalism] (Beijing: Renmin chubanshe, 1985); Fu Yiling, *Ming-Qing shehui jingji bianqian lun* [The transformation of society and economy during the Ming and Qing] (Beijing: Renmin chubanshe, 1989); Fu Zhufu and Li Jingneng, *Zhongguo fengjian shehui nei zibenzhuyi mengya* [The sprouts of capitalism within feudal Chinese society] (Shanghai: Shanghai renmin chubanshe, 1956); Li Wenzhi, Wei Jinyu, and Jing Junjian, *Ming-Qing shidaide nongye zibenzhuyi mengya wenti* [The question of the sprouts of capitalism in agriculture of the Ming-Qing period] (Beijing: Zhongguo shehui kexue chubanshe, 1983); Nanjing Daxue Lishi xi Ming-Qing Yanjiushi, ed., *Ming-Qing ziben-zhuyi mengya yanjiu lunwen ji* [Research papers on the sprouts of capitalism during the Ming and Qing periods] (Shanghai: Shanghai renmin chubanshe, 1981), etc. Working in a different direction, Philip C. Huang has responded to these research conclusions and provided new interpretations in *The Peasant Economy and Social Change in*

North China (Stanford, CA: Stanford University Press, 1985). In the field of intellectual history, Hou Wailu, *Zhongguo sixiang tongshi,* and Xiao Shafu and Xu Sumin, *Ming-Qing qimeng xueshu liubian* [Transformations in Ming-Qing englightenment thought] (Shenyang: Liaoning jiaoyu chubanshe, 1995), etc., have taken roughly similar positions in discussing these issues. Additionally, the "sprouts of capitalism" in the Ming and Qing periods have become important factors in research on *Dream of the Red Chamber (Hong lou meng)* and *Plum in the Golden Vase (Jin ping mei).*

12. Max Weber, *The Religion of China: Confucianism and Taoism,* trans. Hans H. Gerth (New York: Macmillan, 1964). For an analysis of Weber's theoretical perspective and his narrative of Chinese history, see my essay, "Weber and the Question of Chinese Modernity," in Wang Hui, *The Politics of Imagining Asia,* ed. and trans. Theodore Huters (Cambridge, MA: Harvard University Press, 2011).

13. For a useful introduction to debates on "enfeoffment" (*fengjian,* also translated as "feudalism") and centralized administration (*junxian,* also translated as "bureaucratic organization"), see Tu-ki Min, "The Theory of Political Feudalism in the Ch'ing Period," in Tu-ki Min, *National Polity and Political Power: The Transformation of Late Imperial China,* ed. Philip Kuhn and Timothy Brook (Cambridge, MA: Council on East Asian Studies, 1989), 89–136.—Trans.

14. When these narratives enter into interpretations of crises in late nineteenth- and early twentieth-century China or in the contemporary period, certain unspoken conclusions come to the surface in different discourses: first, there is a close relationship between the crisis of modernity in China and the question of whether China can be a unitary state; second, the crisis in China is not some type of crisis of institutions or ideology (such as communism or capitalism), but is a systemic crisis involving all levels of Chinese society; third, internal linkages exist between all aspects of the crisis; these linkages are found in Chinese history or in the past, and thus for China, the only way to escape the crisis is to enact a complete break from its own past. The mutual relationships between these three discourses establish the "totality" of China's crisis, which ultimately is contained within a multifarious "past": Chinese elite culture—including imperial power, the bureaucracy, law, religion—which had already taken shape by the pre-Qin and Qin-Han eras and expanded to an ever greater scale, as well as popular culture,

which had also been deeply influenced and impinged upon by elite culture, all share the same basic characteristics: autocracy (centralized power from the Qin Shihuang to Mao Zedong); cruelty (harsh punishments and strict laws seen in Chinese history); isolation (from the "distinctions between Chinese and foreign" [*yi xia zhi bian*] and the construction of the Great Wall to Mao-era policies of national isolation); and the bureaucracy (from the civil examination system and bureaucracy to the massive organs of the state); etc.

15. See Miyazaki Ichisada, "Song-Yuan shidaide fazhi he shenpan jigou" [The legal system and institutions for examining cases in the Song and Yuan periods], in *Riben xuezhe yanjiu Zhongguo shi lunzhu xuanyi*, 8: 271.

16. Kuhn's research on the Taiping Heavenly Kingdom and local militarization under the Qing opened a new trend in local history in research on Chinese history. See his *Rebellion and Its Enemies in Late Imperial China: Militarization and Social Structure, 1796–1864* (Cambridge, MA: Harvard University Press, 1970). Following this work, a number of historical studies centered on such places as Hankou, Zhejiang, Jiangnan were produced in American scholarship on China.

17. The scholarly perspectives and methods of Liang Qichao, Hu Shi, Hou Wailu, Ying-shih Yu, and Benjamin Elman are all quite different—as are their evaluations of Ming and Qing scholarship—but they nonetheless share a number of common points in the way they view the Ming-Qing transition in relation to modernity. All of their work is concerned with the relationship between elements of Ming and Qing thought and scholarly methods and modernity/capitalism. Examples can be found in Liang Qichao and Hu Shi's praise of the positivist methods found in Qing scholarship; Hou Wailu's research on late-Ming and early-Qing debates from the perspective of "enlightenment" *(qimeng zhuyi);* Ying-shih Yu's discussion of gentry/merchant interactions and the transformation of Confucian thought during the Ming-Qing transition; and in Elman's readings, from the perspective of social history, of the transition from philosophy to philology.

18. See Pamela Kyle Crossley, *A Translucent Mirror: History and Identity in Qing Imperial Ideology* (Berkeley: University of California Press, 1999); Mark C. Elliott, "The Limits of Tartary: Manchuria in Imperial and National Geographies," *Journal of Asian Studies* 59, no. 3 (August 2000): 603–46.

19. See Owen Lattimore, *Inner Asian Frontiers of China* (New York: American Geographical Society, 1940); *Asia in a New World Order* (New York: Foreign Policy Association, 1942).

20. See, for example, Dorothea Heuschert, "Legal Pluralism in the Qing Empire: Manchu Legislation for the Mongols," *International History Review* 20, no. 2 (June 1998): 310–24.

21. Joseph F. Fletcher, *Studies on Chinese and Islamic Inner Asia* (Aldershot, Hampshire, UK: Variorum, 1995).

22. Elliot, "The Limits of Tartary."

23. See Peter Perdue, "Boundaries, Maps, and Movement: Chinese, Russian, and Mongolian Empires in Early Modern Central Eurasia," *International History Review* 20, no. 2 (June 1998): 263–86.

24. Some researchers who study the history of the southwestern areas of the Qing dynasty use the concept of "Chinese colonialism" to describe the Qing's control of the southwest; descriptions of ethnic conflicts in regions with complex ethnic makeups such as Yunnan and Guizhou are often also placed under this same rubric. See Laura Hostetler, "Qing Connections to the Early Modern World: Ethnography and Cartography in Eighteen-Century China," *Modern Asian Studies* 34, no. 3 (2000): 623–62.

25. James Hevia, *Cherishing Men from Afar: Qing Guest Ritual and the Macartney Embassy of 1793* (Durham, NC: Duke University Press, 1995).

26. For example, Zhang Taiyan discussed the relationship between China and ethnicity within an anti-Manchu framework. One essay clearly argues that the period of Manchu rule was a period of history in which China should be seen as a "lost state" *(wangguo)* and refused to accept that the Manchu dynasty had become "Chinese" across 240 years of its rule. See "Zhongxia wangguo erbaisishi'er nian jinianhui shu" [Letter in commemoration of China's 240 years as a lost state], *Zhang Taiyan quanji* [Complete works of Zhang Taiyan] (Shanghai: Shanghai renmin chubanshe, 1985), 188–89.

27. Aside from these other familiar works, Hobson's theory of imperialism has had a deep influence on contemporary discussions of imperialism. His major works include *The Evolution of Modern Capitalism* (London: Walter Scott, 1912); *The War in South Africa: Its Causes and Effects* (New York: Macmillan, 1900); *Imperialism: A Study* (Ann Arbor: University of Michigan Press, 1965); *The Conditions of Industrial Peace* (New York: Macmillan, 1927), etc.

28. For theoretical explanations of imperialism and their contemporary development, see *The Political Economy of Imperialism: Critical Appraisals,* ed. Ronald H. Chilcote (Boston: Kluwer, 1999).

29. Giovanni Arrighi, *The Geometry of Imperialism: The Limits of Hobson's Paradigm* (London: Verso, 1983).

30. See the relevant discussion "The Politics of Imagining Asia," trans. Matthew Hale, appendix 2, in Wang Hui, *The Politics of Imagining Asia,* 10–62.

31. When applied to the Qing dynasty, the term "universal empire" refers not only to the vastness of the dynasty's territory but also to how the dynasty saw itself. Although the Qing empire was ruled by Manchus, who instituted racial hierarchies within the empire and adopted the tribute system and the system of vassal states, this empire saw itself as the ruler of all under heaven *(tianxia)* and did not define its borders or limits according to strict distinctions of inner and outer, whether in terms of territory, race and ethnicity, language, or religion.

32. For a brief discussion of the "provincialization" of Xinjiang, Taiwan, and other frontier territories, see William Rowe, *China's Last Empire: The Great Qing* (Cambridge, MA: Belknap Press, 2009), 210–12.—Trans.

33. For example, Rebecca Karl discusses the emergence of nationalism in China through research on the imagined relationships between modern Chinese revolutions and oppressed peoples of Asia. See her *Staging the World: Chinese Nationalism at the Turn of the Twentieth Century* (Durham, NC: Duke University Press, 2002). Meng Yue's recent book, *Shanghai and the Edges of Empire* (Minnesota: University of Minnesota Press, 2006), traces the contributions made by Yangzhou and Suzhou to the formation of Shanghai's urban culture, examining Shanghai's urban culture and the hybrid relationships between empires. Addressing issues related to translingual practice and translation, Lydia Liu has examined interactions and innovations between Chinese and Western thought; see her *Translingual Practice: Literature, National Culture, and Translated Modernity, 1900–1937* (Stanford, CA: Stanford University Press, 1995).

34. See Wang, *Rise of Modern Chinese Thought,* chapters 7 and 9.

35. See ibid., chapter 10.

36. Mark Elvin, *The Pattern of the Chinese Past: A Social and Economic Interpretation* (Stanford, CA: Stanford University Press, 1973), 17.

2. THE EMPIRE/NATION-STATE BINARY AND EUROPEAN "WORLD HISTORY"

1. Sun Di, *Hongqing jushi ji* [Collection of works by the hermit of Hongqing], juan 9: 21a–b. Wenyuange siku quanshu edition. Other situations arise when the characters *di* and *guo* appear next to one another but do not form a single word.

2. Wang Bo, *Wang Zi'an ji* [Collection of works by Wang Bo] (Shanghai: Shanghai guji chubanshe, 1992), juan 6: 43. [For a brief biography of Sun Quan (182–252), see Rafe de Crespigny, *A Biographical Dictionary of Later Han to the Three Kingdoms* (Leiden: Brill, 2007), 772–74.—Trans.]

3. Chen Pei, "Gongchen lou fu bing xu" [Rhyme-prose on the Gongchen tower with preface], in *Shanxi tongzhi* [Gazetteer of Shanxi province], juan 220.

4. Zhang Weiguo, "Xuan Bangzhi zeng Wang Ershou zuoli kaihe xu," *Wu zhong shuili quan shu* [Collection of works on hydrology in the Wu region], juan 23: 6a. SKQS edition.

5. Wang Tong, *Zhongshuo*, ed. Ruan Yi [Song-dynasty commentator], juan 5: 6b. Sibu beiyao edition.

6. *Tanjin ji* [Tanjin collection], Qisong, ed., juan 6. Wenyuange siku quanshu edition.

7. Huang Zhen, *Huang shi ri chao* [Daily jottings of Mr. Huang], juan 55: 11a–b. Wenyuange siku quanshu edition.

8. The translator has inserted the characters for "empire" (which are the same in Chinese and Japanese) and Chinese and Japanese transliterations to show the overlap of this term across languages.—Trans.

9. Dominic Lieven, *Empire: The Russian Empire and Its Rivals* (New Haven, CT: Yale University Press, 2000), 3. Regardless of whether the concept of "empire" referred to the political entity that, during Roman times, exercised sovereign power within a definite territorial area; or to multinational empires founded on religious or cultural unity, such as the Byzantine Empire, the Muslim world, or the Western Christian world; or even to the global European and American maritime empires of the nineteenth and twentieth centuries, "empire" always implies power and wealth and a unification based on military and cultural power, thus making it a term that received universal approval and even envy. Otherwise, why would the Meiji Japan state, which wanted to

follow in the footsteps of the major European powers, call itself an "empire"? In everyday language, the concept of empire first began to lose its luster as the result of conflicts with the Ottoman Empire and fell even further from favor after the defeat of the "Third Empire" (Third Reich) of Nazi Germany. After World War II, "empire," which was associated with idea of a race-based *Reich,* fell out of general usage. By the time Western societies began referring to the Soviet Union as the "Evil Empire," the negative images carried by this term in its references to the Ottoman Empire and the Third Reich were transferred into an ideological struggle and used as a tool of self-justification by Western democracies. Even so, in cases such as England's naming of itself as the "British Empire" or contemporary references to the United States as the "reluctant empire," the concept of empire still implies power and wealth.

10. S. N. Eisenstadt's 1963 book, *The Political Systems of Empires,* was the first to analyze "empire" as a strict category of political system; it attempted to trace from this analysis the historical roots of democracy and despotism in the nation-state. As a sociologist, Eisenstadt distinguished between different types of empires, with two major types emerging from his analysis: "patrimonial empires" such as the ancient Greek, Incan, and Aztec empires, and "centralized historical bureaucratic empires" represented by China, Rome, Byzantium, the Sassanid Empire, the Islamic caliphate, as well as early European absolutist states. Eisenstadt's book is a structural analysis of types of societies, but it also contains a number of unspoken beliefs about history, especially that the empire was a common political structure before the nation-state. Despite its importance as a work of sociology, few historians have given serious attention to this sociological model of analysis in their narratives of empire or in their use of the concept of empire. See S. N. Eisenstadt, *The Political Systems of Empires* (rpt., New Brunswick, NJ: Transaction, 1993).

11. Jürgen Habermas, "What Is a People? The Frankfurt 'Germanists' Assembly' of 1846 and the Self-Understanding of the Humanities in the *Vormärz,*" in *The Postnational Constelleation: Political Essays,* ed. and trans. Max Pensky (Cambridge, MA: MIT Press, 2001), 9.

12. Perry Anderson, *Lineages of the Absolutist State* (London: Verso, 1979), 397.

13. According to Anderson, "By the 18th century . . . the geographical application of ideas initially conceived in contact with Turkey had

spread steadily further east, in the wake of colonial exploration and expansion: to Persia, then India and finally China. With this geographical extension came a conceptual generalization of the complex of traits initially discerned or confined to the Porte. The notion of political 'despotism' was born. . . ." Ibid., 462.

14. A special explanation of Marx's discussion is needed on this point. In his preface to *A Contribution to the Critique of Political Economy,* Marx argued that the Western historical experience was part of "so many epochs in the progress of the economic formation of society." [See *A Contribution to the Critique of Political Economy,* trans. N. I. Stone (Chicago: Charles H. Kerr and Company, 1918), 13.—Trans.] This preface, however, was never republished after its initial printing (1859), and Marx never again referred to this timeline that later garnered so much attention. A handwritten manuscript (dated August 23, 1857) discovered only after Marx's death was published by Karl Kautsky in *Die Neue Zeit* in March 1903. The English version was first included in the English version of the *Critique of Political Economy* translated by N. I. Stone and published in 1904. In 1877, a Russian scholar argued that, according to "Marxist theory," Russia needed to establish capitalism in order to rid itself of feudalism. According to Marx, his own works offer only a "historical sketch of the development of capitalism in Western Europe," but this sketch cannot be "transform[ed] . . . into a historical-philosophical theory of universal development predetermined by fate for all nations, whatever their historic circumstances in which they find themselves may be. . . . That [view] does me at the same time too much honor and too much insult." See *The Letters of Karl Marx,* ed. and trans. Saul K. Padover (Englewood Cliffs, NJ: Prentice-Hall, 1979), 321.

15. Montesquieu drew connections between empire and the natural environment, especially geography, thus providing a natural basis for accounts of empire—a move that was clearly influenced by the rising tide of scientific narratives from that era. See Montesquieu, *The Spirit of the Laws,* ed. and trans. Anne M. Cohler, Basia Carolyn Miller, and Harold Samuel Stone (Cambridge: Cambridge University Press, 1989).

16. Ibid., 319.

17. Anderson, *Lineages of the Absolutist State,* 400, 412.

18. G. W. F. Hegel, *Philosophy of History,* trans. J. Sibree (New York: Collier, 1900), 111–12.

19. Ibid., 134.

20. Ibid., 164–65.

21. For a discussion of the problem of time in nineteenth-century political economy, see my essay, "Jingji shi, haishi zhengzhi jingji xue?" [Economic history, or political economy?], which serves as an introduction to *Fan shichangde zibenzhuyi* [Against market capitalism], ed. Xu Baoqiang and Qu Jingdong (Beijing: Zhongyang bianyi chubanshe, 2000), 1–49.

22. G. W. F. Hegel, *Elements of the Philosophy of Right*, ed. Allen W. Wood, trans. H. B. Nisbet (Cambridge: Cambridge University Press, 1991), 221.

23. Ibid., 268.

24. In *Elements of the Philosophy of Right*, published in 1821, Hegel divided the development of politics and social organization into three stages. These were the family, civil society, and the establishment of the state: "Civil society is the stage of difference which intervenes between the family and the state, even if its full development occurs later than that of the state; for as difference, it presupposes the state, which it must have before it as a self-sufficient entity in order to subsist itself." Ibid., 220.

25. One can only gain a historically informed understanding of debates about "the end of history" that emerged in the latter part of the twentieth century by placing them in the context of this Hegelian view of history: after a wide variety of diversions an experiments, encounters with tyranny, and nihilism, the concepts of freedom and the democratic state represented by Europe and the relations of production represented by civil society finally return to themselves. See Francis Fukuyama, *The End of History and the Last Man* (New York: Free Press, 1992).

26. Adam Smith, *An Inquiry into the Nature and Causes of the Wealth of Nations* (New York: Modern Library, 1937), 652–55.

27. Ibid., 557.

28. Gellner, *Nations and Nationalism* (Oxford: Blackwell, 1983), 5.

29. Angus Walker, *Marx: His Theory and its Context* (London: Rivers Oram Press, 1978), 64–65.

30. Anderson, *Lineages of the Absolutist State*, 473. Anderson conducted a classic discussion of the Asiatic mode of production, but, for some reason, did not discuss the extremely important influence of Smith and the Scottish school on Hegel's and Marx's ideas about Asia.

31. Anderson, *Lineages of the Absolutist State*, 463.

32. Lenin, "The Awakening of Asia," in *Collected Works* (Moscow: Foreign Languages, 1963), 19: 85.
33. Lenin, "Backward Europe and Advanced Asia," in *Collected Works*, 19: 99.
34. "Democracy and Narodnism in China," in *V. I. Lenin: Selected Works* (New York: International, 1943), 4: 305–6.
35. In mid-nineteenth-century Europe, a fierce debate broke out among Russian elites over the path Russia should take toward modernization, with camps roughly divided into Russian-nativist "Slavophiles" and "Westernizers" who favored the route taken in Western Europe. This "East/West" debate had a deep influence on Lenin and still influences Russian contemporary discussions of reform in Russia. [See note 37 in this section.—Trans.]
36. Lenin, "The Awakening of Asia," in *Collected Works*, 19: 86, 85.
37. Russian intellectuals' views of both Europe and the West were clearly influenced by political developments in early modern Europe and by views of history promoted during the Enlightenment. As used by Lenin, "Asia," a concept closely linked with the concept of despotism, developed from early modern European views on history and politics. For a discussion of the debate between "Slavophiles" and "Westernizers," see the first two chapters of Nicholas Berdyaev, *The Russian Idea*, trans. R. M. French (London: Glasgow Centenary Press, 1947).
38. Lenin, "Democracy and Narodnism in China," in *Selected Works*, 4: 307.
39. Ibid., 4: 310.
40. Lenin, "The Right of Nations to Self-Determination," in *The Lenin Anthology*, ed. Robert F. Tucker (New York: W. W. Norton, 1975), 157.
41. For Lenin, the Asia question was closely connected to the nation-state. He said that, in Asia "the conditions for the most complete development of commodity production and the freest, widest and speediest growth of capitalism have been created only in Japan, i.e., only in an independent national state. [Japan] is a bourgeois state, and for that reason has itself begun to oppress other nations and to enslave colonies." Ibid., 156.
42. Early documents and the Draft Constitution of the Communist Party of China all explicitly made the support for self-determination for ethnic minorities a part of their political program. For example, section 5 of the Basic Law (Constitution) of the Chinese Soviet Republic that was put forward by the Communist Party of China and passed during the First

Plenum of the Central Preparatory Committee for the First National Congress of Workers and Peasants reads: "The fourth major principle of the Basic Law of the Soviet state is to recognize fully and to put into place the right of national self-determination, including the recognition of the right of various minority groups to form separate states. All Mongolians, Hui, Koreans, and other minorities living in Chinese territory are completely free to elect to join the Union of Chinese Soviets or secede from it, and may voluntarily elect to form their own autonomous regions. The Soviet state will work to assist these minority or backward peoples to develop their national cultures and national languages, etc., and will work to help them to develop their economic productivity to produce a material basis close to that of the civilization of the Soviet or of socialism." See *Zhongguo xin minzhuzhuyi geming shiqi genjudi fazhi wenxian xuanbian* [Selection of legal documents from base areas of the revolutionary period relating to new democratic thought in China] (Beijing: Zhongguo shehui kexue chubanshe, 1981), 5.

3. HEAVENLY PRINCIPLE/UNIVERSAL PRINCIPLE AND HISTORY

1. The word *wu* might also be translated as "the material" or "material."—Trans.
2. *Shi,* usually translated as "propensity," has also been translated as "conditions," "historical circumstances," and "conditions of the times." For a detailed discussion of this term in Chinese thought, see Francois Jullien, *The Propensity of Things: Toward a History of Efficacy in China,* trans. Janet Lloyd (New York: Zone Books, 1999).—Trans.
3. Yan Fu, *Tian yan lun* [Discourse on the changes of heaven] (Beijing: Shangwu Yinshuguan, 1981), 92. [For translations of essays by Liu Zongyuan and Liu Yuxi, see H. G. Lamont, "An Early Ninth Century Debate on Heaven: Liu Ts'ung-yüan's *Tien Shuo* and Liu Yü-hsi's *T'ien Lun,* Part I," *Asia Major* 18, pt . 2 (1973): 181–208 and same title, "Part II," *Asia Major* 19, pt. 1 (1974): 37–85.—Trans.]
4. Translation borrowed from Lamont, "An Early Ninth Century Debate," pt. 2, 78. Given his concern for linking evolution and social progress, Yan Fu's greatest concern was the relation between Heaven *(tian)* and social change. According to Liu Yuxi, "Heaven and man predominate in their respective spheres and that is all" (70).—Trans.

5. For one example, we can look to Kang Youwei's exegesis of an important passage from the *Analects*. The original passage reads: "Zi Gong said: 'While I do not wish others to impose on me, I wish not to impose on others either.' The Master said: 'Si, that is quite beyond you.'" According to Kang: "Zi Gong desired to not have others impose on him, this [is a desire for] independence and liberty. To not impose on others means not violating others' independence and liberty. Humans are born from Heaven/Nature *(tian)*, and when all are subject to Heaven/Nature, then all are independent and free. Each person has boundaries, and if he violates others' boundaries, then he puts pressure on others' independence and liberty; this is entirely contrary to the Universal Principle *(gongli)* determined by Heaven/Nature and is unacceptable. Zi Gong had heard of the learning of independence and liberty found in the Way of Heaven; in order to perfect the Universal Principle of the Way of humans, he hoped to spread this learning to all under Heaven. Because Confucius was born in a time of great disorder, [his thinking] was still undeveloped; although the Way [he advocated] was perfect, he tried to put it into practice too early [in history] . . . if a time of peace was reached he would be able to put it into practice." Kang Youwei, *Lunyu zhu* [Commentaries to the *Analects*], ed. Lou Yulie (Beijing: Zhonghua shuju, 1984), 61. [Translation of passage from Confucius borrowed from *The Analects,* trans. D. C. Lau (Hong Kong: Chinese University Press, 1992), 41.—Trans.]

6. The rites/music system *(li yue zhidu)* flourished in the Shang and Zhou periods and reached its height in the Western Zhou; it is said that this system was established by the Duke of Zhou. The rites/music system divides rites (ritual) and music into two mutually interconnected parts. "Rites" mainly works to regulate human identity through the forms of rituals and institutions. According to the *Book of Rites,* for example, "They are the rules of propriety [*li*], that furnish the means of determining (the observances toward) relatives, as near and remote; of settling points which may cause suspicion or doubt; of distinguishing where there should be agreement, and where difference; and of making clear what is right and what is wrong." It also states: "The course (of duty), virtue, benevolence, and righteousness cannot be carried out without the rules of propriety . . . nor can the (the duties between) ruler and minister, high and low, father and son, elder brother and younger brother, be determined." [Translation borrowed

from *The Lî Kî,* trans. James Legge, in *The Sacred Books of the East* (rpt., Delhi: Motilal Banarsidass, 1966), vol. 27: 63.] Based on the relationships established by ritual propriety, music is used in a way that is adjusted according to the status of different individuals, so that at events such as sacrifices, feasts, weddings, and funerals, varying instruments and types of music were played according to the status and rank of those involved. The many aspects of the rites/music system, the system of enfeoffment *(fengjian zhi),* and the patriarchal clan system *(zongfa zhi)* all combined to form the order of classical Chinese society. To use ritual propriety *(li)* to govern the state meant using ritual propriety to determine positions and status within hierarchies and using music to harmonize relationships between people in order to achieve an ideal, harmonious order. In Confucian political formulations, the rites/music society represented an ideal social order.

7. See Wang, *Rise of Modern Chinese Thought,* chapters 8 and 11.

8. Hans-Georg Gadamer, *Reason in the Age of Science,* trans. Frederick G. Lawrence (Cambridge, MA: MIT Press, 1988), 6.

9. Alasdair MacIntyre, from the Chinese preface to *After Virtue: A Study in Moral Theory,* trans. Gong Qun and Dai Yongyi (Beijing: Zhongguo shehui kexue chubanshe, 1991), 1. [The original English version of this preface could not be located, so it was back-translated from the Chinese.—Trans.]

10. See Wang, *Rise of Modern Chinese Thought,* chapter 11.

11. See ibid., chapter 1.

12. *Han Changli wenji jiaozhu* [Annotated collection of the prose of Han Yu], ed. Ma Qichang (Shanghai: Shanghai guji chubanshe, 1986), 9.

13. For a capsule description of commentaries to this trigram, see *The I Ching,* trans. Richard Wilhelm and Cary Byrnes (Princeton, NJ: Princeton University Press, 1950), 200–204. Translation of *Mencius* borrowed from *Mengzi: With Selections from Traditional Commentaries,* trans. and ed. Bryan W. Van Norden (Indianapolis, IN: Hackett, 2008), 132.—Trans.

14. Cheng Hao and Cheng Yi, *Zhouyi Cheng shi zhuan* [The Cheng brothers' commentaries to the Book of Changes] (Beijing: Zhonghua shuju, 1981), 3: 921.

15. See SKQS edition of *He ding ce bu Da Yi ji yi cui yan,* ed. Nalan Xingde, juan 11: 10. This and the previous quotation also appear in a

Yuan collection by He Bingwen, *Si shu tong*, "Mengzi tong" section, juan 3, 6a. SKQS edition.

16. He Bingwen, *Si shu tong* [Comprehension of the Four Books], "Mengzi tong" [Comprehension of Mencius], section, juan 3: 6a. SKQS edition.

17. *Zhanguo ce zhushi* [Annotated Edition of *Stratagems of the Warring States*], ed. He Jianzhang (Beijing: Zhonghua shuju, 1990), 419. Translation modified from Bramwell Seaton Bonsall, *Records of the Warring States*, http://lib.hku.hk/bonsall/zhanguoce/12.pdf (accessed April 4, 2013).

18. Zhang Dai, *Zhang Dai ji* [Collection of works by Zhang Dai] (Beijing: Zhonghua shuju, 1978), 205.

19. Zhu Xi, *Si shu huo wen* [Questions and answers on the Four Books], in *Zhu zi quan shu* [Complete works of Master Zhu Xi], ed. Zhu Jieren et al. (Shanghai: Shanghai guji chubanshe, 2002), 6: 948.

20. Translation borrowed from *The Lî Kî*, trans. James Legge, in *The Sacred Books of the East* (rpt., Delhi: Motilal Banarsidass, 1966), vol. 27: 396.—Trans.

21. For a translation of the relevant passages and discussion of this terminology, see William H. Nienhauser et al., *Liu Tsung-yüan* (New York: Twayne, 1973), 54–55, 126. Translations and information on the official titles *fangbo* and *lianshuai* are found in Charles O. Hucker, *A Dictionary of Official Titles in Imperial China* (rpt., Taipei: SMC, 1985), 209, 311–12.—Trans.

22. See Wang, *Rise of Modern Chinese Thought,* chapter 1.

23. These quotations refer to the opening lines of *The Great Learning*, a section from the *Book of Rites (Li ji)* promoted to the level of a "classic" (*jing*) by the great Song-dynasty philosopher Zhu Xi (1130–1200). The complete text of the passage is as follows: "The way of the Great Learning lies in clearly manifesting luminous virtue, renewing the people, and resting in the utmost good. Knowing where to rest [stop], there is stability; with stability, one can have composure; with composure one can be at peace; at peace one can deliberate [reflect], and with reflection one can get there [understand]." Translation borrowed from *Sources of Chinese Tradition*, ed. William Theodore de Bary, 2nd ed. (New York: Columbia University Press, 1999), 725–26.—Trans.

24. See Wang, *Rise of Modern Chinese Thought,* chapter 4.

25. See ibid., chapter 3.

26. For a translation Zhang's essay with this famous statement, see Zhang Xuecheng, *On Ethics and History: Essays and Letters of Zhang Xuecheng*, ed. and trans. Philip J. Ivanhoe (Stanford, CA: Stanford University Press, 2010), 25–44.—Trans.

27. For a brief summary of Gu Yanwu's views, see On-Cho Ng and Q. Edward Wang, *Mirroring the Past: The Writing and Use of History in Imperial China* (Honolulu: University of Hawaii Press, 2005), 229–31.—Trans.

28. See Wang, *Rise of Modern Chinese Thought*, chapter 2.

29. In explaining the question, "What is meant by 'learning to become a great person' *(da ren zhi xue)* and investigating into roots and branches of affairs and events?" Wei Yuan replied: "In the making of one's intentions, every thought and consideration are part of it. In the making of one's heart-mind, the Four Sprouts *(si duan)* and Five Natures *(wu xing)* are all part of it. In the making of one's body, the Five Matters and Five Cardinal Relationships are all part of it. In the making of the state, tens of thousands of considerations are a part of it. Who would enjoy the grace of the Emperor on High without principle or nature?" In this explanation we again see the breadth of the category of "things and affairs" *(wu)*. See "Mo gu," in *Wei Yuan ji* [Collection of Wei Yuan's works] (Beijing: Zhonghua shuju, 1976), 1: 4.

30. Translation modified from Wing-tsit Chan, *Instructions for Practical Living and other Neo-Confucian Writings by Wang Yang-ming* (New York: Columbia University Press, 1963), 243.—Trans.

31. For a discussion of the two-tax system, see *Cambridge History of China*, Vol. 3: *Sui and T'ang China*, ed. Denis Twitchett, (Cambridge: Cambridge University Press, 1979), pt. 1: 581.—Trans.

32. See Miyazaki and Naitō, in *Riben xuezhe yanjiu Zhongguo shi lunzhu xuanyi*, 1: 10–18, 153–241.

4. CHINA'S MODERN IDENTITY AND THE TRANSFORMATION OF EMPIRE

1. This line of argument works to show that China lacks the internal forces that would move it toward a democratic society or to imply that the progress of capitalism will lead China to political dissolution. See Lucian W. Pye, *The Spirit of Chinese Politics* (Cambridge, MA: MIT Press, 1968), xviii.

2. W. J. F. Jenner argues that, compared with English and other European languages, Chinese is a backward, primitive written language naturally suited to autocratic tradition, and that history written in this language is not only a "history of tyranny" but the "tyranny of history." See Jenner, *The Tyranny of History* (London: Penguin Press, 1992). Just as arguments that place historical studies in China in the same position as European religion are rooted in nineteenth-century missionary historiography, arguments that seek to explain China's unity and conservatism through comparisons between Chinese and European languages are also inherited from nineteenth-century European missionaries. For example, in his *The National Life of China* (Edinburgh, 1862), R. H. Patterson analyzed the relationship between the isolationism of the Chinese empire and its geographical isolation, noting specifically that this situation also bore some relation to the unique aspects of "their written language."

3. Jenner, *Tyranny of History,* 249.

4. See Benedict Anderson, *Imagined Communities: Reflections on the Origin and Spread of Nationalism* (London: Verso, 1991).

5. Ibid.

6. According to Burkhardt, "What is of more importance is the general and undisputed respect for pure language and pronunciation as something precious and sacred. One part of the country after another came to adopt the classical dialect officially." *The Civilization of the Renaissance in Italy,* trans. S. G. C. Middlemore, 2nd ed. (London, 1890), 380.

7. Karatani Kōjin, "Nationalism and Écriture," trans. Indra Levy, *Surfaces* 201 (1998): 5.

8. Kang Youwei, "Jiaoxue tongyi: yanyu" [General discussion on education: on language], *Kang Youwei quanji* [Complete works of Kang Youwei] (Shanghai: Shanghai guji chubanshe, 1987), 159. [Here Kang refers to the use of unofficial, and sometimes confusing and pedantic, terms for divisions of land and administration, as well as the practice of using archaic names to refer to specific areas of China, e.g., *Qin* instead of Shanxi.—Trans.]

9. For a detailed discussion, see my "Local Forms, Vernacular Dialects, and the War of Resistance Against Japan: The 'National Forms' Debate," trans. Chris Berry, in Wang Hui, *The Politics of Imagining Asia,* ed. Theodore Huters (Cambridge, MA: Harvard University Press, 2011), 95–135.

10. Using China as his example, Prasenjit Duara has argued that national identity is a phenomenon that already existed in premodern times; it is a product of the effects of mutual interactions between history and memory. It is not "print capitalism," but the historically situated hybrid products of myth, written language, and spoken language that form the primary media for the imagining the Chinese nation. According to Duara, "It was not only, or perhaps even primarily, the print media that enabled Han Chinese to develop a sharp sense of the Other, and hence of themselves as a community, when they confronted other communities." See Duara, *Rescuing History from the Nation: Questioning Narratives of Modern China* (Chicago: University of Chicago Press, 1995), 53.

11. Politics and business are the greatest forces for unifying language (as seen in the Putonghua movement from the 1950s and in the decline of education in minority languages) as part of the process of moving to a market economy. This process is universal around the world, but the social conditions and means by which they take place vary greatly. For example, when compared with the "Russification" polices of Tsar Alexander II of the mid-nineteenth century, the situation in China described in this section is quite different.

12. Wilhelm von Humboldt, *On Language: On the Diversity of Human Languages,* ed. Michael Losonsky, trans. Peter Heath (Cambridge: Cambridge University Press, 1992), 219.

13. Hu Sansheng's commentary on the 108th juan of the *Zizhi tongjian* [Comprehensive mirror for aiding governance] reads: "From the Sui dynasty onwards, among those who gained fame and renown, seven or eight out of ten were from Daibei [i.e., the northern and northwestern border regions]." When describing the influence of the Xianbei language, the "Words and Sounds" *(ci yan)* section of the *Yan shi jia xun* [Family instructions for the Yan clan] said, "The south is colored by Wu and Yue, and in the north [the people] are mingled with the northern barbarians."

14. Zhang Taiyan, "Zhonghua Minguo jie" [The meaning of the "Republic of China"], *Zhang Taiyan quanji* [Complete works of Zhang Taiyan] (Shanghai: Shanghai renmin chubanshe, 1985), 4: 252–62.

15. Some scholars have argued that the political culture of the Yuan dynasty was based on a "duality of Mongol and Han," by which the Yuan made use of existing Han practices while preserving "national [Mongol]

customs"; while the Yuan adopted Han rituals, official and military institutions, and the tax and corvee system, they also retained and promoted Mongol institutions such as the *kheshig* imperial guards, *appanage* (Ch: *touxia*) fief distribution, etc. The main difference from the Qing dynasty is that the Mongolian language always served as the language of officials in the Yuan, so many Mongol emperors spoke only Mongolian and no Chinese. See Li Zhi'an, Wang Xiaoxin, eds., *Yuan shi xue gai shuo* [Outline of the historiography of the Yuan dynasty] (Tianjin: Tianjin jiaoyu chubanshe, 1989), 4.

16. See Wang, *Rise of Modern Chinese Thought,* chapter 5.

17. Karl Marx, *The Communist Manifesto: The Centenary Edition,* ed. Harold Laski (London: Allen & Unwin, 1948), 125. The building and rebuilding of the Great Wall has frequently been used to describe China's supposed isolationist tendencies because orthodox Chinese thought has in fact often used this man-made construction and tool of war as a dividing line between inner and outer. Using the ancient Great Wall as a metaphor for China's isolationism, however, one will encounter unexpected difficulties. Owen Lattimore's analysis of the Great Wall is an excellent example of the complexities involved.

18. Owen Lattimore, *Inner Asian Frontiers of China* (New York: Oxford University Press, 1940).

19. These connections changed over time, and thus it was not always the same part of the world that shared these connections with China. See Jacques Gernet, *Le Monde Chinois* (Paris: Armond Colin, 1990), 26.

20. See Wang, *Rise of Modern Chinese Thought,* chapters 3 and 5.

21. See ibid.

22. See ibid., chapter 8.

23. See ibid., chapter 3.

24. See ibid., chapters 5 and 6.

25. On numerous occasions Kangxi dispatched representatives to Japan to seek trade opportunities, all of which failed because of Japan's isolationist policies. After the pacification of Taiwan in 1683, officials overseeing the borders in the southeastern provinces requested that the sea ban be lifted, to which Kangxi immediately assented. In 1685, Kangxi opened four major customs stations for international trade: Macau (in Guangdong), Zhangzhou (in Fujian), Ningbo (in Zhejiang), Yuntaishan (in Jiangsu). He subsequently announced an end to duties on ships from Holland and Siam, and reduced duties on commercial trade from

elsewhere. The opening of ports in Jiangsu, Zhejiang, Fujian, and Guangdong during Kangxi's reign, the signing of the Treaty of Kyakhta by the Yongzheng emperor, and commerce between the Qing and Korea, Vietnam, and Southeast Asia all demonstrate that the Qing did not merit the accusations of isolationism that were later directed at it.

26. The Qianlong emperor did issue an order limiting foreign trade to Canton (Guangzhou); forbidding foreign trade in Xiamen, Ningbo, and other locations; and increasing import duties.

27. See Wang, *Rise of Modern Chinese Thought,* chapter 6.

28. For an account in English, see Sima Qian, *Records of the Grand Historian: Han Dynasty,* trans. Burton Watson (New York: Columbia University Press, 1993), pt. 1: 437–39.—Trans.

29. In this anecdote, Duke Wen of Jin promised to complete the invasion of Yuan within ten days. By the end of that time, Yuan had not been fully conquered, but his officers recommended that he stay to complete the operation. According to the *Han Feizi,* "In response, the Duke said: 'I set the time limit to my men at ten days for the expedition. If I do not leave, I will violate faith with my men. Taking Yuan and thereby breaking faith, I cannot bear.' So saying, he stopped the campaign and left. Hearing about this, the people of Yuan said: 'Such a faithful ruler they have! How can we refuse to turn to him?'" Translation modified from *The Complete Works of Han Fei Tzu: A Classic of Chinese Political Science,* trans. W. K. Liao (London: Probsthain, 1959), 2: 59–62.—Trans.

30. See Wang, *Rise of Modern Chinese Thought,* chapter 8.

31. Elie Kedourie, *Nationalism,* 3rd ed. (London: Hutchison, 1966), 126–27.

32. Anthony Smith, *Nations and Nationalism in a Global Era* (Cambridge: Polity Press, 1995), 99.

33. Smith, *Nations and Nationalism in a Global Era,* 101–2.

34. Alexis de Tocqueville, *The Ancien Régime and the French Revolution,* trans. Gerald Bevan (New York: Penguin, 2008), 45–53.

35. Karl Marx, *The Eighteenth Brumaire of Louis Bonaparte* (New York: International, 1963), 15, 16.

36. Vladimir Ilyich Lenin, "Democracy and Narodnism in China," in *V. I. Lenin: Selected Works* (New York: International, 1943), 4: 310.

37. Ernest Gellner, *Nations and Nationalism* (Ithaca, NY: Cornell University Press, 1983), 84–85.

38. See Wang, *Rise of Modern Chinese Thought,* chapters 3 and 7.

39. See ibid., chapters 7, 8, 9.

40. See ibid., chapter 8.

41. See ibid., chapter 9.

42. See ibid., chapter 10.

43. See Michael Hardt and Antonio Negri, *Empire* (Cambridge, MA: Harvard University Press, 2000).

Index

Absolute Spirit, 49; Hegel on, 45–46; historical stages of, 46
Academies for Correct Pronunciation, 106
Agrarian society, 48
American Revolution, 70
Ancient learning movement, 105
Anderson, Benedict, x; on nationalism, 103
Anderson, Perry, 39, 52
Antihumanism, 95–96
Arrighi, Giovanni, 22
Asia: characteristics of, 41–42; history lacking in, 42; despotism and, 42–43; as civilizational form, 43; as starting point, 45; Lenin on, 54–55, 159n41
Asiatic mode of production, 52
Assimilation model, 35
Authoritarianism, 136
"Awakening of Asia, The" (Lenin), 54

"Backward Europe and Advanced Asia" (Lenin), 54
Bacon, Francis, 22
Benjamin, Walter, 103
Berman, Harold J., 9–10
Bodin, Jean, 39–40

Book of Changes, x; propensity of times in, 74
Book of Great Unity, The (Kang), 97
Book of Rites, 161n6, 163n23
Bourgeois society, 15
Braudel, Ferdinand, 22
Bukharin, N. I., 22
Burkhardt, Jacob, 104–105

Capitalism, 5; print, x; sprouts of, 11, 14, 150n11; Ming dynasty, 14; Song dynasty, 14, 92–93; colonialism and, 20; industrial, 20; mercantilist, 20; finance capital and, 22; imperialism and, 22; Lenin on, 58; modernity and, 89–90
"Casting off Barbarians" (Wang Fuzhi), 120
Centralization, 133; power, 132–143; new identity model for, 134–135; modernity and, 139. See also Decentralization
Centralized administration (junxian zhi), 14, 33; Song dynasty as, 36; Liu Zongyuan on, 77; Qing dynasty, 125; introduction to debates on, 151n13
Chen Yinke, 18

171

Cheng Yi, 74, 75
Chinese identity: language problems and, 104–114; Confucianism and, 114–124; in minority-rule dynasties, 114–124
Citizen rights, 132
Civilizational difference theories, 5, 11
Civilization of the Renaissance in Italy, The (Burkhardt), 104–105
Civil society, 47; Hegel on, 158n24
Clan institutions, 134–135; limiting power of, 135; social mobilization and, 136
Classics: propensity of times and, 81; study of, 140
Class relations, 101
Collection of Writings by the Hermit of Hongqing (Sun Di), 30–31
Colonialism: historical confusion over, 18; premises of, 18; Qing dynasty, 18–21, 153n24; broadening of term, 20; industrial capitalism and, 20; mercantilist capitalism and, 20; characteristics of, 23–24; Adam Smith on, 50–51
Commercial society, 48, 50
Communist Party of China Draft Constitution, 159n42
"Concerning Armies" (Qisong), 32
Confucianism: Weber's analysis of, 5; necessity of power and, 74–75; Song dynasty, 91; Chinese identity and, 114–124; in minority-rule dynasties, 114–124; racial distinctions of, 117–118. *See also* Neo-Confucianism; Orthodoxy
Continuity myth: legitimacy through, 102; orthodoxy and, 117, 132
Contribution to the Critique of Political Economy, A (Marx), 157n14
Cultural identity, 3

Culturalism, 5, 42, 102
Cyclical dynasty model, 15

Daily Accumulation of Knowledge (Gu Yanwu), 126
Daily Jottings of Master Huang (Huang Zhen), 32–33
Dai Zhen, 79
Decentralization, 17
"Democracy and Narodnism in China" (Lenin), 54
Despotism: Oriental, 40, 50, 52–53; Asia and, 42–43
Discontinuity, ix, 72
"Distinctions between Barbarians and Chinese" (Lü Liuliang), 120
Doctrines of the Middle Way (Wang Tong), 32
Dong Zhongshu, 122
Dragon descendants, 101–102
Du Yaquan, 68
Duara, Prasenjit, 166n10
Dzungars, 17

East Asian modernity, 15; Kyoto School and, 7–10
Eastern and Western Cultures and their Philosophies (Liang Shuming), 6–7
Eastern Orthodox Church, 10
East India Company, 128, 129
Eisenstadt, S. N., 156n10
Elements of International Law (Wheaton), 130
Elvin, Mark, 26–27
Emperor: Five Emperors, 31–33; First, 34; Kang Youwei on, 123–124, 131
Emperor's Four Treasuries, 74
Empire, 3–4, 17–18; post–Roman Empire, 24–25; etymology of, 30; multiple meanings of, 30–33; Five

Emperors and, 31–32; three levels of, 33; virtue and, 33; misgivings regarding, 35; Lieven on, 37; devaluation of, 37–38; characteristics of, 40–41; Montesquieu on, 42, 157n15; Qing dynasty, 154n31; universal, 154n31; implications of, 155n9

Empire of Great Japan, 33–34

Enfeoffment (*fengjian zhi*), 13, 14, 33; Liu Zongyuan on, 77, 90; introduction to debates on, 151n13

Enlightenment, 11, 40, 152n17; modernity and early, 89–90

Ethnic identity, 17–18; transformation of, 115; Qing dynasty prohibitions, 118–119, 121; Anthony D. Smith on, 135–136. *See also specific ethnic identities*

Europeanized writing, xiii

European nationalism: condemnation of, 4; Kedourie on, 133–134

Evidential learning, 112–113

Evidential Studies of the Meanings of Characters in the Mencius (Dai Zhen), 79

Evolution, 98–99

Evolution and Ethics (Huxley), xii

Fairbank, John K., 4, 5, 6

Fengjian zhi. See Enfeoffment

Feudal society, 48

Fichte, Johann Gottlieb, 141

First Emperor, 34

Five Emperors, 33; empire and, 31–32

Five Nations Under One Union, 131–132

Fletcher, Joseph F., 17

Folk culture, 7

Foreign Affairs Movement, 119–120

Foreignization, 115

Four Categories of Literature (*si bu*), 81

French Revolution, 40, 70; Tocqueville on, 137; Marx on, 138

Frontier style, 118

Fukuzawa Yukichi, 54

Gazetteer of the Maritime States (Wei Yuan), 127–128

Gellner, Ernest, 51; on nationalism, 139–140

Geographical studies (*yudi xue*), 126–128, 130–131

German world, 46

Germany: Nazi, 37–38, 155n9; Habermas on, 38–39; nation-state, 38–39; metaphysical tradition, 44–45

Gernet, Jacques, 114, 118

Globalization, xi, 142–143

Gong Zizhen, 126

Grand unification, 116

Great Wall: Lattimore on, 117; Marx on, 117; as center, 118; isolationism and, 167n17

Greek world, 46

Gumplowicz, Ludwig, 22

Gu Yanwu, 63, 67–68, 80–82, 88, 121, 126; Kang compared with, 140

Guo Xiang, 78

Habermas, Jürgen, 38–39

Halde, Jean Baptiste Du, 42

Han identity, 112; Qing dynasty and, 18–19, 120–122; Qing dynasty encouraging immigration of, 19; as national identity, 27; dynasty characteristics, 36–37; fantasy of pure, 115; Manchu identity relationship with, 120–121, 125; Zhang Taiyan on, 141; Mongols and, 166n15

Han Yu, 71, 74

Heart-mind, 86–87; learning, 67, 68
Heavenly Principle: discontinuity and, ix, 72; Kyoto School and, ix; May Fourth Movement and, ix; protomodern nationalism and, ix; secularism and, ix; translation problems, xi–xii; religion and, 62; legitimacy and, 64–65, 91; background on, 71–72; rupture and, 72–73; propensity of times and, 73–74; lacking understanding of, 83; Universal Principle and, 86–100; incompatibility with modernity, 87; problems emphasized by, 90–91; institutions and, 94–97; ideal society and, 96
Hegel, G. W. F., xii–xiii, 41; on language, 44–45; on Absolute Spirit, 45–46; philosophy of history, 45–50; world history framework of, 45–50; on nomadic peoples, 51; on civil society, 158n24
Hengqu's Discussions on the Book of Changes (Zhang Dai), 75
Hereditary aristocracy, 7
Hilferding, Rudolph, 21–22
Hitler, Adolf, 22
Hobson, J. A., 21–22; on imperialism, 153n27
Hou Wailu, 86–87
Hu Sansheng, 166n13
Hu Shi, 86–87
Huang Zhen, 32–33
Huang Zongxi, 88
Humboldt, Karl Wilhelm von, 111–112
Huxley, Thomas, xii, 63
Hybridity, 25–26; of Qing dynasty, 36

Ideal society, 96
Identity: cultural, 3; from within, 6; Chinese, 104–124; centralization and

new model for, 134–135; Mongol, 166n15. *See also* Ethnic identity; Han identity; Manchu identity; National identity
Imagined communities, x, 3, 28, 104; dependency factors, 103
Imagined Communities (B. Anderson), 103
Imperialism: European, 4; Qing, 18–21, 24–25; causes behind, 21–22; values of, 21–22; benefits of, 22; capitalism and, 22; economic resources to discuss, 22; groupings of human beings and, 22; long-term historical perspective on, 22–23; violence and, 23; characteristics of, 23–24; Lenin on, 54; international relations and, 124–132; sovereignty and, 124–132; territorial expansion and, 124–132; disintegration of, 137; Hobson on, 153n27. *See also* Authoritarianism
Industrial capitalism, 20
Industrial Revolution, 128–129
Intellectual history, 86
Intellectual traditions, 93
International law, 130–131; ancient, 12–13
International relations, 124–132
Investigating things and extending knowledge (*gewu zhi zhi*), 83–85, 93–94
Isolation, 165n2; Great Wall and, 167n17; of Japan, 167n25

Japan: Empire of Great, 33–34; War of Resistance against, 108–110; Lenin on, 159n41; isolationism of, 167n25
Jenner, W. J. F., 165n2
Jin dynasty, 116
Junxian zhi. See Centralized administration

Kang Youwei, 26, 93, 97; on language, 106–107; on emperor, 123–124, 131; Gu Yanwu compared with, 140
Kant, Immanuel, 141
Karl, Rebecca, 154n33
Kautsky, Karl, 22
Kedourie, Elie, 133–134
Kingly transformation, 35–36
Kōjin Karatani, 105
Kuhn, Philip, 16, 152n16
Kyoto School: Heavenly Principle and, ix; East Asian modernity and, 7–10; nationalism and, 8–9

Land reform, 57
Language, x; Hegel on, 44–45; nationalism and, 103; Chinese identity and problems of, 104–114; reform movements, 105; Kang on, 106–107; internationalist orientation in, 108; modernity and, 108; Humboldt on, 111–112; national characteristics defined by, 111–112; human spirit influenced by, 112; shared, 113
Latinization movement, 109
Lattimore, Owen, 16–17; on Great Wall, 117
Learning: Heart-mind, 67, 68; unadorned, 67; ancient, 105; evidential, 112–113; New Text, 116, 121, 123–124; statecraft, 140
Legitimacy: Heavenly Principle and, 64–65, 91; Universal Principle and, 64–65; through continuity myth, 102; of Jin dynasty, 116; of Qing dynasty, 116–117; orthodoxy and, 117
Lenin, Vladimir, 22; on revolution, 53–56; on imperialism, 54; on Asia, 54–55, 159n41; on self-determination, 55, 57–58; on

Narodnism, 56–57; historical dialectics of, 57; on capitalism, 58; on nation-state, 58; on Japan, 159n41
Levenson, Joseph R., 5
Li Zhi, 86, 88
Liang Qichao, 26, 68, 86–87, 93; on open nationalism, 141
Liang Shuming, 6–7
Lieven, Dominic, 37
Linking three systems, 116–117
Lin Zexu, 127–128
Liu, Lydia, 154n33
Liu Fenglu, 121
Liu Yuxi, 63–64
Liu Zongyuan, 63–64; on centralized administration, 77; on enfeoffment, 77, 90; on propensity of times, 77–78
Lü Liuliang, 120
Lu Xiangshan, 63, 75
Lu Xun, 93
Lu Zuqian, 74
Luxemburg, Rosa, 22
Luxuriant Dew of the Spring and Autumn Annals, 121, 122

Machiavelli, Niccolo, 22; on Turkey, 39
Manchu identity, 17; expansion of, 14, 21; Han identity relationship with, 120–121, 125; lost state and rule of, 153n26; Zhang Taiyan on, 153n26
Mandate of Heaven, 77
Mao Zedong, 27, 93
Maritime networks, 128
Marx, Karl, 41, 157n14; economic structure of society by, 52–53; on revolution, 54; on Great Wall, 117; on French Revolution, 138
May Fourth Movement, 91, 107; Heavenly Principle and, ix; internationalist tendencies of, 110

"Meaning of the 'Republic of China,'
The" (Zhang Taiyan), 113–114
"Memorial Written to Congratulate the
Emperor on His Ascent to the
Throne Today," 30–31
Meng Yue, 154n33
Mercantilist capitalism, 20
Military industrialization, 128
Ming dynasty capitalism, 14
Missionary descriptions, 12
Miyazaki Ichisada, 7; on Yuan dynasty
legal code, 15
Modernity, 1–2; achievements of, 5;
from within, 6; Opium Wars and, 6,
13; East Asian, 7–10, 15; origins of,
10, 14; premature demise of early, 11;
elements of, 13; antithesis of, 13–14;
signs of, 13–14; Qing dynasty and, 14,
16; entangled, 25–26; Heavenly
Principle incompatible with, 87; rise
of, 87; neo-Confucianism and, 88–89;
capitalism and, 89–90; early
enlightenment and, 89–90; intellectual traditions and, 93; antihumanism
and, 95–96; nature and, 98; nation-
state as innovation of, 103; language
and, 108; centralization and, 139;
Russia and, 159n35
Modern market society, 48
Mongol identity, 166n15
Montesquieu, 41; on empire, 42,
157n15; on natural, 157n15
Morality, 90
Moral philosophy, 10
Moral relationships, 66
Multipolarity, 17
Mussolini, Benito, 22

Naitō Konan, 7
Narodnism, 138–139; Lenin on,
56–57

National identity: as Han identity, 27;
class relations and, 101; orthodoxy
and, 101; modes of interpreting,
101–103; print culture and, 111;
citizen rights and, 132; Duara on,
166n10
Nationalism, x; protomodern, ix;
European, 4, 133–134; cultural, 6;
political, 6; Kyoto School and, 8–9;
self-determination and, 17, 137;
Benedict Anderson on, 103; language
and, 103; spread of, 103; vernacular,
104–105; phonocentrism and,
105–106; in central Europe, 133–134;
Kedourie on, 133–134; normalization
of, 139; Gellner on, 139–140; Liang
Qichao on, 141
National Language Romanization
movement, 105–106
Nation-state, 4; transformation of,
28–29; German, 38–39; Habermas
on, 38–39; Lenin on, 58; as innovation of modernity, 103; shared
cultural essence and, 113; competition between, 130–131
Naturalism, 63–64
Nature, 98–99; control of, 98; denaturalization of, 98; modernity and, 98;
as objective, 98; imagined, 102–103
Nazi Germany, 37–38, 155n9
Neo-Confucianism: distinctions in, 67;
challenges to, 68; natural and, 78;
propensity of times and, 78–83;
modernity and, 88–89; self-negating
tendencies, 95–96; criticism of, 140
New Culture, 91, 107
New Text learning, 116, 121, 123–124
Nietzsche, Friedrich, 141

October Revolution, 55, 56
"On Enfeoffment" (Liu Zongyuan), 90

Opium trade, 128
Opium Wars, 4; modernity and, 6, 13; acceptance of Western knowledge after, 16; treaties signed following, 129–130
Oriental despotism, 40, 50; characteristics of, 52–53
Orthodoxy, 116; break from, 72–73; national identity and, 101; continuous development of, 117, 132; legitimacy and, 117

Patterson, R. H., 165n2
People's Republic of China, 137
Phonocentrism, 105; nationalism and, 105–106
Polanyi, Karl, 22
Political Systems of Empires, The (Eisenstadt), 156n10
Positivism, 152n17
Power: lordly, 40; Confucianism and necessity of, 74–75; centralization, 132–143; clan institutions limited, 135
"Preface to the Writings of Xuan Bangzhi Presented to Vice Magistrate Wang Upon Channeling the Yellow River" (Zhang Guowei), 31
"Preface Written at a Banquet in at the Home of Wu Shaofu of Jiangning, A" (Wang Bo), 31
Premodern concepts, ix
Prince, The (Machiavelli), 39
Print: capitalism, x; culture, 111
Production and reproduction, x, 78
Propensity of principle, 75–77
Propensity of times, 61–86; Heavenly Principle and, 73–74; in *Book of Changes*, 74; in *Emperor's Four Treasuries*, 74; propensity of principle replacing, 75–77; Liu

Zongyuan on, 77–78; neo-Confucianism and, 78–83; classics and, 81
Property inheritance, 134
Protestant ethics, 43
Protomodern nationalism, ix
Provincialization, 154n32

Qin Shi Huang, 34
Qing dynasty: modernity and, 14, 16; Han identity and, 18–19, 120–122; colonialism, 18–21, 153n24; imperialism, 18–21, 24–25; Han immigration encouraged by, 19; tribute system, 25; hybridity of, 36; characteristics of, 36–37; overthrow of, 53–54; legitimacy of, 116–117; ethnic prohibitions by, 118–119, 121; inner and outer distinctions, 118–120; centralized administration of, 125; sea ban by, 128; universal empire and, 154n31
Qisong, 32
Qu Qiubai, 109

Racial characteristics, 26; Confucianism and, 117–118
Rationalization: Weber on, 11–12, 43; economic, 12; origins of, 12; political, 12, 13; Protestant ethics and, 43
Records of Great Righteousness Resolving Confusion, 120
Religion, 62
Republic of China, 113–114
Revolt of the Three Feudatories, 125
Revolution: French, 40, 70, 137, 138; Lenin on, 53–56; Marx on, 54; October, 55, 56; American, 70; Industrial, 128–129
"Revolution in China and Europe" (Marx), 54

"Rhyme-Prose of Taking Pity on
    Myself" (Han Yu), 74
"Rhyme-Prose with Preface on the
    North Star Tower" (Chen Fei), 31
Ricardo, David, 21–22
Rites and music system, 72, 73, 81–82,
    161n6
Roman Catholic Church, 10
Roman Empire, 24–25
Roman world, 46
Royal sovereignty, 40
Ruling nations, 22
Russia, 37–38, 155n9; modernity and,
    159n35

Scientific knowledge, 40, 68–69
Secularism, ix
Self-criticism, 7
Self-determination, 39, 53–54;
    nationalism and, 17, 137; Lenin on,
    55, 57–58; political, 58; Communist
    Party of China Draft Constitution
    and, 159n42
Sibree, John, xii–xiii
Sinicization, 115
Six Arts, 81, 97
Smith, Adam, 21–22, 23, 41; economic
    history by, 48–49; on nations of
    hunters, 50; on European coloniza-
    tion of Americas, 50–51
Smith, Anthony D., 135–136
Society for Unified Pronunciation,
    106
Song dynasty: capitalism, 14, 92–93; as
    centralized administration, 36;
    Confucianism, 91
Sovereignty: Bodin on, 39–40; royal,
    40; imperialism and, 124–132
Spencer, Herbert, 63
Statecraft learning, 140
Stimulus-response model, 4, 5

Style problems, 149n11
Sun Di, 30–31
Sun Yat-sen, 26, 27, 93; land reform
    program, 57

Taiping Rebellion, 16, 125, 152n16
Tang dynasty, 36–37
Tang-Song transformation, 7
Theory of Heaven, 63–64
"Theses on the Philosophy of History"
    (Benjamin), 103
Three Dynasties of Antiquity, 71–72;
    rites and music of, 72, 73, 81–82;
    ideal of, 78; as fiction, 102
Time: as space, 45–46; propensity of,
    61–86; linear, 63; timeless sense
    of, 102
Tocqueville, Alexis de, 137
Transformations of heaven, 64
Translation problems, viii, xi–xiv;
    Heavenly Principle, xi–xii; Universal
    Principle, xi–xii
Treaty of Kyakhta, 127, 167n25
Treaty of Nerchinsk, 127
Treaty system, 129–130
Tribute system, 129–130; Qing, 25
Tropes of equivalence, viii
Turkey, 155n9; Machiavelli on, 39

Unity, 115–116
Universal empire, 154n31
Universal Principle, ix, x, 59–60;
    translation problems, xi–xii; disinte-
    gration of, 62; legitimacy and, 64–65;
    establishment process of, 68–69;
    epistemology and, 69–70; Heavenly
    Principle and, 86–100; ideal society
    and, 96; Zhang Taiyan on, 96

Violence, 23
Virtue, 33

Walker, Angus, 51
Wang Anshi, 90
Wang Bo, 31
Wang Fuzhi, 120
Wang Gen, 86
Wang Ji, 86
Wang Tong, 31–32
Wang Yangming, 86, 88
Wang Zaoshi, xii–xiii
War of Resistance against Japan, 108–109; revival of local culture during, 109–110
Warring States period, 131
"Way of Great Centrality" (Liu Zongyuan), 90
Wealth inheritance, 134
Wealth of Nations, The (A. Smith), 50
Weber, Max: Confucianism analysis of, 5; on rationalization, 11–12, 43
Wei Yuan, 119–121, 127–128
Western Territories, 126
Wheaton, Henry, 130

Will of Heaven, 34
World history: Eurocentric narratives of, 6–8, 43–45; Hegel on, 45–50; end of, 52; starting point, 52

Yan Fu, 63–64, 68, 93; translations by, 141
Yuan dynasty, 15

Zarrow, Peter, xii
Zeng Jing, 120
Zhang Dai, 75
Zhang Guowei, 31
Zhang Taiyan, 26, 93; on Universal Principle, 96; on Republic of China, 113–114; on Han identity, 141; on negative utopia, 141–142; on Manchus, 153n26
Zhang Xuecheng, 63, 81–82; on Dao, 81
Zhang Yongle, 147n2
Zhu Xi, 64, 75, 78, 88, 163n23
Zhuang Cunyu, 121